EAT MORE, BURN MORE

EAT MORE,
BURN MORE:

STUFF YOUR FACE, STILL LOSE WEIGHT

CHEF GUI ALINAT

Early To Rise
HEALTH, WEALTH AND A LIFE WELL LIVED

Library of Congress Control Number: 2015914245

Early To Rise Publishing
14405 W Colfax Ave #309
Lakewood, CO 80401
www.earlytorise.com

ISBN: 978-0-9967389-0-3

Ordering Information:
Quantity sales. Special discounts are available on quantity purchases by corporations, associations, and others. For details, contact the publisher at the address above.

The information included in this book is for educational purposes only. It is not intended nor implied to be a substitute for professional medical advice. The reader should always consult his or her healthcare provider to determine the appropriateness of the information for their own situation of if they have any questions regarding a medical condition or treatment plan. Reading the information in this book does not create a physician-patient relationship.

Eat More, Burn More is a registered trademark of Early To Rise Publishing, LLC.

Printed in the U.S.A.
Photography by: Chef Gui Alinat
Book design and layout by: Stewart A. Williams

Alinat, Gui
Eat More, Burn More: Stuff Your Face, Still Lose Weight

First Edition

"Chef Gui has catered numerous parties for me, and as a fitness professional, I'm always looking to serve food that's both healthy and delicious to my guests. Chef delivers both! Even better, now you personally have the opportunity to access all these same fat-burning "secret" recipes for you and your family. Your taste buds will rejoice as your waistline shrinks. Highly recommended!"

—JOEL MARION, 4-time Bestselling Fitness Author

CONTENTS

ACKNOWLEDGEMENTS ~ 9

INTRODUCTION ~ 11

SPECIAL INSTRUCTIONS ~ 14

BREAKFAST ~ *17*

APPETIZERS ~ *49*

MAIN COURSES ~ *91*

SIDES ~ *179*

SNACKS ~ *209*

INDEX ~ 232

ACKNOWLEDGMENTS

This book is dedicated to my children: Julian, Brooke, Brune, Bradley, and Scarlett. I truly hope the cruel exposure to braised exotic meats, Brussels sprouts, or leafy green vegetables, will lead you to a life of fitness, conviviality, and cultural awareness.

I want to thank my wife, Carissa Alinat, for always being on my side, and giving me the strength and motivation when I needed it most. You are the most talented, loving, and dedicated person I know. Thank you also for putting up with a constant activity in the kitchen, and makeshift photo studios in our home.

This book would not even exist without my friends Craig Ballantyne and Joel Marion, the two famed fitness experts who took me under their wings. This is the beginning of a great relationship and for that, I am forever indebted to you both.

Finally, I want to thank my local friends who helped the making of this book by testing and tasting some recipes, providing feedback, and overall being encouraging and awesome: Eileen Thornton, Guillaume Gruet and Sandy Kisslinger, Charlotte Embody, Damien McKinney, Patrick Artz, and my dedicated staff Veronica Waldo, Salwa Berrada, Monica Findlay, and Miranda Furlan.

INTRODUCTION

So you want to have your cake and eat it too? I can't blame you. Who *isn't* interested in 'stuffing' their face with great tasting food without suffering the consequences often associated with it?

I'm glad you're interested in this cookbook. We already have something in common. Controlling your weight, building defining muscles, and enjoying a healthy body you can be proud of is at the top of your priority list. It's at the top of mine too.

CHEF!

My name is Gui Alinat. Everybody calls me 'Chef,' though, because for the past 23 years, I have dedicated my life to the craft of cooking awesome, healthy food that makes people happy.

When I'm not in my catering kitchen in Tampa, Florida, you'll find me cooking for my large family. My wife Carissa and I have five children, and we often joke that every family dinner is like a catering event, except we don't get paid for it! I cook in large batches, kids help with their chores, and we all have fun preparing the meal together.

I cook for my catering clients and for my family, and regular meals for nutrition expert Joel Marion and his family. It's a lot of fun to cook for his adorable family and all of their friends. But when you cook for someone who has had so much success in the nutrition industry, you have to know what you're cooking! My job is to make sure his family, like mine, enjoys wholesome, healthy meals.

My wife Carissa and I take our family dinners seriously. The epidemic of obesity and cardio-vascular diseases in the United States is strong and very real. However, we can do something about it by choosing to prepare healthy meals.

AN INSPIRATION

I was born, raised, and formally trained as a chef in the South of France, where the Mediterranean Sea provides a bounty of opportunities for awesome food and a very healthy lifestyle. I'm sure you've heard about the Mediterranean Diet. It's become a buzzword over the years. More than a diet or lifestyle, it's a real way of life, backed by scientific research. In a nutshell, living the Mediterranean way is simply sharing the values adopted by countries like Greece, Italy, Spain, and the South of France––a lifestyle of soft exercise and food consumption that is fresh, healthy, and delicious.

As a child in the South of France, I don't remember anyone being preoccupied with dieting. People simply concentrated on what to cook and eat for dinner (and a very late dinner at that!). It was always about the enjoyment of great food. A celebration of life, if you will. It was like being on a permanent vacation. We walked to the busy outdoor market, caught up with friends we ran into, and planned our meals based on whatever ingredients were fresh and in season. If the eggplants, zucchini, basil and tomatoes looked good, then we had ratatouille for dinner. If we came across a particularly fresh fish? We grilled and paired it with ratatouille. "Oh, and look how mature this goat cheese looks?" someone might say. Discussions at the outdoor market revolved around eating. Meal plans involved fresh vegetables, some healthy protein, whole grain carbohydrates, fiber, and there was always room for the most nutritious ingredients. Red wine flowed, and we stayed for hours at the dinner table, lingering and socializing among family and friends. What glorious experiences!

Times have changed, however. We're all busier now and often in a hurry. It's not always easy to make time for long walks to the market or hours-long meals with your buddies. I get that. I love remembering those times, however, and get inspired by the Mediterranean way of life. I believe that everyone should have the same opportunity I had to enjoy the gift of great food and health at the same time.

WHAT'S IN IT FOR YOU?

I love my weight, my body, and my lifestyle. I feel great most of the time, and I get things done. I'm energized, healthy, and very happy. I do exercise, and promote it to my children. But as you know, exercise is only half the equation. The other half comes from the food you eat. As it turns out, enjoying awesome-tasting, fat-burning foods that offer the best of both worlds is possible. Do not compromise on that, and don't let anyone tell you otherwise. You *can* have everything, and you can have it all at once. Remember, you want to have your cake and eat it too!

My mission today is to work for you, to give you the experience of having your own private chef. I've made the commitment to help you and thousands of good folks like you to enjoy the gift of healthy food that tastes great. So you can 'stuff your face' and still be fit!

I chose my best 100 comfort food recipes and stripped them of anything that makes it difficult for you to control your weight. I tweaked recipes for you. I packed super foods wherever I could. I counted calories, cut down on fat, added lots of ingredients loaded with fiber, vitamins, minerals, and overall goodness. I identified what was wrong with the ingredients and techniques we all crave. I got rid of troublemakers, substituted, and re-engineered the recipes in such a way that you are now free to enjoy these foods without worry or guilt.

Go ahead. Make cooking at home your workout. All the recipes are super fast and uninvolved. Gather ingredients, chop, sizzle, and move around your kitchen. Everything is designed to make cooking easy and fun. You might also burn calories as you cook.

Food is linked to health and happy living. It inspires, delights, and fulfills us. Food is about enjoyment, not compromise. As a chef, I am always focused on superior taste. It's what drives me. And I want you to see what this delicious food can do for you.

You can trust a skinny chef! You won't gain weight by eating this wholesome food. You can be confident that by providing you with easy-to-make, fat-burning recipes, I've taken care of half of your weight control problems. Now you can stick to your plan, focus your efforts on exercise, and succeed.

SPECIAL INSTRUCTIONS

My cooking philosophy relies on simple, wholesome, natural ingredients. I avoid processed items. As you peruse this book, you may come across unfamiliar ingredients or question why I use certain things. I'm happy to explain my reasoning and my choices.

GOING ORGANIC

The health of my family is important to me so we select organic ingredients whenever possible. I say 'whenever possible' because sometimes we compromise. I believe it is highly beneficial, but it's not always possible, practical, or budget-friendly to insist on a strict, one hundred percent organic diet. I was joking the other day with my chef buddy Dr. BBQ about organic poppy seeds we found at a local grocery store. Who feels the need to pay twice the price for an item used maybe twice a year?

EMPTY CALORIES

Many of the foods and beverages Americans eat and drink contain empty calories, which are fats and added sugars offering few or no nutrients. I fight these with a passion, and you should hear my kids complain about it (our house is a candy/soda/junk-free zone). In this book, I tried to replace empty calorie ingredients with items that provide a nutritional benefit.

FIBER

There is much scientific evidence that fiber really is the undervalued nutrient we all need, and it has a beneficial impact on weight control. That's why I tend to add fiber-loaded ingredients to my recipes: leafy green vegetables, flax seeds, coconut or buckwheat flours, whole grain pasta, etc. It makes a huge difference.

COOKING PASTA AL DENTE

This is a healthy chef secret. Cooking pasta al dente plays a beneficial role in your diet, especially if you're trying to burn fat. Simply follow the cook time instructions on the package. I even take one or two minutes off that time to enjoy pasta the way the Italians do in Italy.

REPLACING SUGARS

Our family avoids sugar. The evidence against sweets is overwhelming. Most refined sugars offer nothing beneficial and in fact, accelerate weight gain. I promote natural sugars present in fresh and dried fruits. I replace white sugar with honey or molasses because of their lower glycemic index. Sometimes, recipes calling for sugar do better with Truvia®, a commercial name but a natural sweetener coming from the leaves of the stevia plant. Truvia® is MSG-free, GMO-free, and gluten-free.

REPLACING REFINED FLOUR

White flour raises your blood sugar and triggers weight gain. It also makes you feel tired and unproductive. For those reasons, it's best to substitute and use flours that bring fiber, promote fat loss, and don't make you feel tired or sleepy after eating.

The problem is wheat flour contains gluten, which makes the dough chewy and well, dough-ey. A good dough is sometimes difficult to achieve with alternative flours. Coconut flour and buckwheat flours, for instance, do not contain gluten. Therefore, they result in a dough that is not as chewy and soft as traditional wheat flours. To get the results I want, I usually choose a combination of coconut, buckwheat and whole grain flours, which gives me the best of both worlds.

OLIVE OIL

Not all olive oil is created equal. We know by now that extra-virgin, first cold pressed, olive oil is the way to go. To take it one step further, choose the best olive oil your money can buy—estate olive oil, which is produced by a variety of families or micro-factories, not processed by the big brand companies. This has some importance because fraud can be an issue (some so-called olive oil, in fact, is not), and because small estates have much better control of the quality.

DEEP-FRYING

I consider deep-frying (cooking something in a large amount of hot oil) counterproductive in a fat loss or bodybuilding diet. For recipes with a four-serving yield, about ten percent of the cooking oil is retained in the food you eat. This can't possibly be good news. Instead, I promote baking/roasting or broiling to reproduce the golden crust of deep-fried items.

SHOCKING INGREDIENTS!

You may recognize 'bad' ingredients in some recipes that you would not use otherwise. Yes, I do use cheese, cornstarch, breading, and some fat and sugary items from time to time. When I do, the recipe is engineered in such a way that the amounts are minimal and do not impact your fat loss efforts.

EQUIPMENT

This cookbook is all about helping you make a quick start. I tried to limit the amount of pantry ingredients and equipment you'll need. My goal is to make this cookbook universal and within reach of everyone. For most of the recipes, all you need is a good cutting board (I recommend a large, thick, stable wooden cutting board), some good German or Japanese knives, and a set of reliable pots and pans (I recommend cast iron skillets and Dutch ovens). One last piece of equipment I could not live without—a hand blender. It allows you to emulsify sauces and dressings, blend soups right in the pot, and really limits clean up.

BREAKFAST

BELGIAN WAFFLES

Active time: 15 minutes | **Cook time:** 10 minutes | **Yield:** 4 servings

INGREDIENTS:

¼ cup coconut flour

½ cup whole-wheat flour

⅛ cup buckwheat flour

⅛ cup ground flaxseed

1 tbsp honey

1 tsp baking powder

¼ tsp ground cinnamon

⅛ tsp salt

¾ cups fat-free milk

¾ tbsp butter, melted

¾ tbsp unsweetened applesauce

1 large egg, lightly beaten

½ large ripe banana, mashed

cooking spray

No need to top your waffles with a ton of whipped cream. Instead, go with a ton of fresh fruits, and a little maple syrup. My waffles are thick, wholesome, full of fiber and nutrients, and will start your day the right way with something delicious and healthy!

PREPARATION:

1. Combine flours, flaxseed, honey, baking powder, cinnamon and salt in a medium bowl, stirring with a whisk.
2. Combine milk, butter, applesauce, and eggs, stirring with a whisk; add milk mixture to flour mixture, stirring until blended. Fold in mashed banana.
3. Preheat a waffle iron. Coat iron with cooking spray. Spoon about ¼ cup batter per 4-inch waffle onto hot waffle iron, spreading batter to edges. Cook 3 to 4 minutes; repeat procedure with remaining batter.

OLD-FASHIONED PANCAKES

Active time: 10 minutes | **Cook time:** 10 minutes | **Yield:** 4 servings

INGREDIENTS:

½ cup coconut flour

½ cup whole grain flour

½ tbsp honey

½ tsp baking soda

½ tsp baking powder

½ tsp ground cinnamon

¾ cups low-fat buttermilk

⅔ tbsp melted butter

⅓ tsp vanilla extract

6 large eggs

1 large, ripe banana, mashed

A pinch of salt

I once knew a short order cook who could make pancakes that looked like photos of the faces of the four Beatles singing group. You could actually recognize John Lennon, Paul McCartney, Ringo Starr, and George Harrison. Chances are you won't try to mimic the cook's artistry but you can enjoy eating these mouth-watering pancakes in any shape you choose.

QUICK TIP: Using a funnel, pour batter into squeeze bottles. That way you can control how much batter to put on the pan. Even better, kids love squeezing pancake batter, making faces, writing stuff, or drawing Mickey's big ears.

PREPARATION:

1. Combine flours, honey, baking soda, baking powder, cinnamon, and salt in a large bowl; stir with a whisk.
2. Combine buttermilk, oil, vanilla, and eggs; add to flour mixture, stirring until smooth. Fold in banana.
3. Spoon ¼ cup batter per pancake onto a hot nonstick pan. Turn when tops are covered with bubbles and edges look cooked. Be gentle while flipping pancakes over.
4. Serve pancakes with pure maple syrup.

EASY BANANA BREAD

Active time: 8 minutes | **Cook time:** 1 hour | **Yield:** 4 servings

INGREDIENTS:

¼ cup unsweetened applesauce

⅓ cup honey

1 egg, beaten

1⅔ bananas, finely crushed

⅓ cup coconut flour

½ tsp baking soda

¼ tsp salt

¼ tsp vanilla

Every family has a banana bread recipe. In my family, it's this easy-to-make, wholesome and tasty bread that kids will love, thanks to the sweet banana flavor.

QUICK TIP: For a quick addition, add walnuts or pecans.

PREPARATION:

1. Preheat oven at 350° (180°c). Mix together applesauce and honey. Add eggs and crushed bananas. Combine well.
2. Sift together flour, baking soda and salt. Add to the mixture. Add vanilla. Pour into greased and floured loaf pan.
3. Bake at 350° (180°c) degrees for 60 minutes. Let cool at room temperature, then refrigerate.

TIME SAVER: Make sure you use the muffin cups, and spray the pan and cups with cooking spray for easy removal.

SERVING INFO: 420 calories, 16g fat, 66g carbohydrates, 8g protein, 8g fiber, 45g sugar

BLUEBERRY MUFFINS

Active time: 10 minutes | **Cook time:** 15 minutes | **Yield:** 4 servings

INGREDIENTS:

¼ cup butter

¼ cup applesauce

½ cup honey

1 large egg

½ tsp vanilla

1 tsp baking powder

¼ tsp salt

⅓ cup coconut flour

⅓ cup buckwheat flour

⅓ cup whole
grain flour

¾ cup low-fat milk

1½ cups blueberries

Sometimes, simplicity is key. In fact, in my kitchen simplicity is key *most* of the time. I choose wholesome ingredients, a quick and easy recipe to display those ingredients, and that's it.

QUICK TIP: Use frozen blueberries if fresh are not an option in your area. Be sure to add them to the batter in their frozen state or you'll end up with very purple muffins.

PREPARATION:

1. Preheat oven to 375° (190°c) and grease muffin cups. In a bowl, mix butter, applesauce, and honey. Add egg, vanilla, baking powder, salt, and beat.
2. With a rubber spoon, fold in half of flour then half of milk into batter; repeat. Fold in blueberries. Spoon into muffin cups.
3. Bake 15 to 20 minutes, until golden brown and springy to touch.

TIME SAVER: Make sure you use the muffin cups, and spray the pan and cups with cooking spray for easy removal.

SERVING INFO: 182 calories, 0g fat 5

SPINACH AND TOMATO FRITTATA

Active time: 10 minutes | **Cook time:** 20 minutes | **Yield:** 4 servings

INGREDIENTS:

4 eggs, beaten

8 egg whites, beaten

1 tsp extra-virgin olive oil

1 cup chopped spinach

1 cup tomatoes, diced

1 cup chopped ham

1 tbsp chopped cilantro leaves

1 tbsp chopped garlic

salt and pepper to taste

This is a true story. One day I was invited to a potluck. Thirty minutes prior to leaving my house, I still hadn't decided what to bring. I opened the fridge and found eggs and a bunch of loose ingredients here and there, which are now the main items in this recipe! I grabbed a pan, cooked the eggs with spinach, tomato, ham, and a few seasonings, and took the pan to the potluck. This last-minute dish was the hit of the meal. Everyone asked me for the recipe. Sometimes things work that way. Chefs are really good at putting miscellaneous ingredients together. Here is one recipe that allows you to do just that.

QUICK TIP: This is your opportunity to be creative. Add cheese, deli meat, herbs, and whatever vegetable you have in your refrigerator, etc.

PREPARATION:

1. Preheat oven to broil setting. In a medium size bowl whisk together eggs, egg whites, spinach, ham, tomatoes, salt and pepper.
2. Heat a 12-inch non-stick, oven safe sauté pan over medium high heat. Add oil and pour egg mixture into pan and stir with heat-resistant rubber spatula. Sprinkle with garlic and parsley.
3. Place pan into oven and bake for 15 minutes, until lightly browned and fluffy. Remove from pan and cut into 4 servings. Serve immediately.

OPTIONS: For variety and another dimension, add sundried tomatoes. They pair very well with the spinach. Also try lean cheese such as goat or feta.

SERVING INFO: 270 cal · 12g fat · 54g carbohydrat · 12g protein · 6g fiber · 25g su

FRENCH TOAST

Active time: 20 minutes | **Cook time:** 10 minutes | **Yield:** 4

INGREDIENTS:

8 slices unsweetened, whole-grain bread (Such as Ezekiel's)

2 tbsps honey

2 tbsps vegetable or coconut oil

3 eggs

2 egg whites

¼ cup milk

½ tsp vanilla extract

¼ cup pure maple syrup

1 tsp ground cinnamon

¼ tsp ground nutmeg

Surprisingly, French Toast is not popular in France. It is, however, very popular in my family of seven. I cook most of the meals at home, but Carissa likes to handle breakfast, especially on weekends, and French Toast is a favorite. What makes this recipe special? The type of bread you use. Choose a real whole grain, unsweetened bread with a variety of grains and seeds. That makes this recipe wholesome and nutritious. Next, spice the egg mixture just right and select egg whites instead of whole eggs.

QUICK TIP: If you can find artisan whole grain bread that is unsliced, you may want to give it a try. Slice it thick and proceed with the recipe. It makes a beautiful difference.

PREPARATION:

1. In a small bowl, combine cinnamon, nutmeg, and honey and set aside briefly.
2. Whisk together cinnamon mixture, eggs, milk, and vanilla and pour into a shallow container such as a pie plate.
3. In skillet, heat up oil at medium heat. Dip bread in egg mixture. Add slices to the pan and cook until golden brown, then flip to cook the other side.
4. Serve with syrup.

HUEVOS RANCHEROS

Active time: 15 minutes | **Cook time:** 20 minutes | **Yield:** 4 servings

INGREDIENTS:

1 small can whole peeled tomatoes

¼ cup fresh cilantro leaves, plus more for garnish

½ onion, diced

1 clove garlic, peeled and smashed

1 jalapeno pepper (seeded if desired)

vegetable oil or coconut oil

four 6-inch corn tortillas, plus more for serving, optional

1 small can refried beans

8 egg whites

1 avocado, pitted, peeled and diced, for garnish

⅓ cup crumbled queso fresco, for serving

Read my lips. There is NO BETTER breakfast recipe than Huevos Rancheros. Now, do you have any further questions? The truth is, this classic Mexican breakfast is absolutely delicious, and very close to my heart. I spent a lot of time in Mexico. I explored the country from Guatemala to the US border, and from Cancun to Acapulco, visiting most of the historical sites and museums, eating in fancy restaurants and from street food carts alike, and meeting hundreds of local folks along the way. One of my very best friends has been living for years in the tiny coastal village of San Agustinillo, along the Pacific Ocean. I still visit him and his adorable family from time to time, and breakfast revolves around either Eggs ala Mexicana, or Huevos Rancheros. Imagine that: a wholesome, rustic tortilla, spread with refried beans, topped with eggs, a delicious tomato-chili sauce, fresh avocado and cilantro.

QUICK TIP: Wear plastic gloves when handling chili peppers.

PREPARATION:

1. In a food processor, combine the tomatoes, cilantro, onions, garlic, jalapeno, and salt; puree until smooth.

2. Transfer the sauce to a small skillet and simmer over medium heat until slightly thickened, about 10 minutes. Cover and keep warm over low heat.

3. Wrap tortillas with a clean, lightly moist cloth. Microwave on high approximately 1 minute, or until hot and pliable. Transfer each one to an individual plate.

4. Heat the refried beans, in a small saucepan. Spread the beans on the tortillas.

★ FAV ★

5. Add a tbsp of oil to a skillet. Working in batches of 2, crack the eggs into the skillet. Cook until the bottoms are set and the edges golden, 1 to 2 minutes. Turn the heat to medium-low, cover and cook until set, about 1 minute more. Place 1 egg on each tortilla and spoon the warm sauce over the eggs. Sprinkle with the avocado, cheese, and additional cilantro.

15-MINUTE TIMESAVER: You can make a quick version of the sauce with your favorite salsa. Just blend it and heat it up. Then start the recipe at step 3 (or step 4 if you don't mind tortillas at room temperature).

SERVING INFO: 450 calories, 24g fat, 26g carbohydrates, 24g protein, 8g fiber, 18g

SPANISH TORTILLA

Active time: 25 minutes | **Cook time:** 30 minutes | **Yield:** 4 servings

INGREDIENTS:

4 tbsps extra-virgin olive oil

4 cups onions, sliced

2 lbs. rutabaga, peeled and cubed (about 4 cups)

7 eggs, beaten

7 egg whites, beaten

½ cup finely diced ham

3 tbsps snipped fresh chives

salt and pepper to taste

When I was a young sous-chef, I found a job in a Spanish restaurant. It was tough trying to make Spanish tortilla! The local chef wanted it to be thick and cooked uniformly, never too brown, and never too pale. It had to taste good whether warm or cold. Finally, I made the recipe easy and foolproof. I replaced the usual potatoes with rutabaga. A vegetable with a similar texture and taste that burns fat.

QUICK TIP: Conveniently, Spanish tortilla can be served warm, chilled, or at room temperature.

PREPARATION:

1. In a sauté pan over medium heat, add the oil and cook the onions until slightly caramelized, about 20 minutes.
2. Meanwhile, add the cubed rutabaga to a saucepan, and fill up with water until it reaches the top of the rutabaga. Bring to a simmer and cook until fork tender, about 15 minutes. Then drain.
3. Add the rutabaga to the onions and finish cooking until golden brown, stirring occasionally, about 10 minutes.
4. Mix the eggs and egg yolk, and salt and pepper to taste. Fold the onion, potatoes, and ham into the eggs. Pour the entire mixture into the hot pan and cook, undisturbed, until the bottom is set and the top is still runny, about 10 minutes. Continue to cook until the bottom is lightly golden, using a rubber spatula to run around the edge of the eggs, lifting slightly to allow the eggs to run to the bottom and cook.
5. When the top of the tortilla begins to set, place a large plate or serving platter on top of the skillet and, working quickly, invert the tortilla onto the plate. Carefully slide the tortilla back into the skillet so that the browned side is now facing up. Cook until the bottom is golden brown, 10 minutes longer.
6. Remove the tortilla from the skillet and serve hot, warm, or at room temperature. To serve, cut the tortilla into thin wedges. Garnish with fresh chives.

SERVING INFO: 350 calories, 11g fat, 21g carbohydrates, 13g protein, 2g fiber, 0g sugar

GREEN EGGS MEXICANA

Active time: 5 minutes | **Cook time:** 10 minutes | **Yield:** 4 servings

INGREDIENTS:

1 tbsp extra-virgin olive oil

2 cups salsa verde

8 large egg whites

½ cup queso fresco

½ cup chopped fresh cilantro leaves

2 large 8-inch sprouted grain tortillas such as Ezekiel's

salt to taste

Another fat-burning recipe from Mexico! With a 15-minute total time, this may very well become your favorite.

QUICK TIP: You'll most likely find salsa verde in the international section of your grocery store. It is made out of green tomatillos, jalapeno peppers and cilantro. It's somewhat spicy but still mild.

PREPARATION:

1. Preheat the oven to 400° (200°c). Lightly oil an ovenproof dish. Place the 2 tortillas at the bottom. Pour the salsa into the dish, on top of the tortillas.
2. Break the eggs onto the salsa. Season with salt. Bake until the egg whites turn opaque and are cooked, about 10 minutes.
3. Sprinkle the cheese over the eggs and continue baking until just melted, about 2 minutes more. Top with the cilantro and serve immediately.

STEEL-CUT OATMEAL AND FRUITS

Active time: 2 minutes | **Cook time:** 15 minutes | **Yield:** 4 servings

INGREDIENTS:

1½ cups steel-cut whole grain oatmeal

2 cups low-fat milk

2 tbsps sliced almonds, toasted

1 cup blueberries

1 tsp fresh ginger, minced

2 tsps honey

1 tsp flaxseed

2 tbsps plain Greek yogurt

Why steel-cut whole grains? Because they're a nutritional powerhouse. A whole grain of oat has all of its nutritional health benefits. Processed grains lack the bran and germ because they are removed during the milling process. That really is too bad, because most of the nutrients are in the bran and germ: dietary fiber, iron, and B vitamins.

We know how important fiber is for weight control. My oatmeal recipe makes a delicious, wholesome, chewy, hot cereal that provides lasting energy all morning. It's a great way to start your day and add fiber to your diet.

QUICK TIP: Steel-cut oats take longer to cook than instant oats (but have a much better glycemic index). However, presoaking them will cut down a lot of the cooking time.

PREPARATION:

1. Bring milk to a boil. Add oats, reduce heat, and cook 10-20 minutes, depending on the consistency you desire.
2. Stir in the almonds, ginger, honey, blueberry, and flaxseed. Top with yogurt, and serve.

MY EGGS FLORENTINE

Active time: 15 minutes | **Cook time:** 15 minutes | **Yield:** Serves 4

INGREDIENTS:

3 tbsps extra-virgin olive oil

1 lb. baby spinach

½ onion, roughly chopped

1 clove garlic, minced

1 tbsp coconut flour

½ cup low-fat milk

3 ounces Neufchâtel cheese

Pinch of freshly grated nutmeg

4 eggs or 8 egg whites

salt and pepper to taste

Did you know the word 'Florentine' is part of the classic French cooking repertoire and designates a recipe containing spinach? Over time, chefs well-versed in French cooking terms would add the word 'Florentine' to any dish served on a bed of spinach, including eggs. Today this delicious breakfast classic is served everywhere. You'll be delighted with this version of Eggs Florentine. It's super easy to make and delicious.

QUICK TIP: Spinach should be cooked to the very minimum. Just let it wilt (it will greatly decrease in volume) in a hot pan, and that's it. Do not overcook and it will remain bright, green, and full of flavor.

PREPARATION:

1. Preheat the oven to 350° (180°c).
2. Melt 1 tbsp of olive oil in a large sauté pan over medium heat. Quickly wilt the spinach. Season with salt and pepper and place the spinach in a colander over a bowl to drain.
3. Add 2 tbsps of oil to the pan. When hot, add the onion and garlic and cook over medium heat until the onion is translucent and tender, about 5 minutes. Add the flour and cook, stirring, for 1 minute. Gradually whisk in the milk and, while whisking constantly, bring to a boil, about 3 minutes. Add the Neufchâtel cheese, nutmeg, and salt and pepper. Once the sauce has thickened, remove it from the heat and continue to whisk for 1 minute more.
4. When the spinach has cooled, squeeze out any excess liquid, coarsely chop, and add to the warm sauce. Stir well to combine.
5. Spread the spinach mixture in an even layer in the bottom of a baking dish. Using a spoon, make 4 wells in the spinach for the eggs. Pour 1 egg or 2 egg whites into each well. Bake until the spinach is warmed through and the eggs are set and cooked to the desired degree of doneness, about 15 minutes. Serve warm.

FAV

5-MINUTE TIMESAVER: Skip the wilting of the spinach by using frozen spinach, and start the recipe at step 3. Fresh is better, but frozen spinach will get you were you want to go, fast.

OPTIONS:
1. Try this recipe with kale or Swiss chard for a change.
2. Neufchatel is similar to cream cheese, but leaner. You may substitute it for cream cheese.

SERVING INFO: 240 calories, 16g fat, 10g carbohydrates, 13g protein, 4g fiber, 4g sugar

SERVING INFO: 250 calories, 11g fat, 20g carbohydrates, 18g protein, 5g fiber, 3g sugar

THE GOOD WRAP

Active time: 15 minutes | **Cook time:** 10 minutes | **Yield:** 4 wraps

INGREDIENTS:

4 taco-sized whole grain tortilla (such as Ezekiel's)

4 tbsps hummus (from page 219)

4 eggs

4 egg whites

½ cup red onions, chopped

8 cups baby spinach

4 tbsps goat cheese, crumbled

4 tbsps sun-dried tomatoes, chopped

hot sauce, for topping

salt and pepper to taste

I can't get enough of this wrap! I know it's *unusual,* but the combination works very well. It's easy, fast, and nutritious and especially convenient when you're in a hurry. Wrap up this breakfast and go!

QUICK TIP: Make your own hummus (recipe page 219).

PREPARATION:

1. Add just enough extra-virgin olive oil to coat a medium skillet. Sauté onions in the skillet over medium-high heat until soft and translucent, about 3-4 minutes.
2. Add spinach and wilt.
3. Whisk eggs and egg whites, and add them to the pan with vegetables, to cook until eggs are cooked through, about 2 minutes. Add salt and pepper to taste.
4. Spread a layer of hummus on the tortilla. Place the egg scramble in the center of the tortilla and sprinkle with sun-dried tomatoes and goat cheese. Add hot sauce, if using.
5. Fold the tortilla and serve.

BANANA-QUINOA PORRIDGE

Active time: 10 minutes | **Cook time:** 15 minutes | **Yield:** 4 servings

INGREDIENTS:

1 cup whole grain quinoa

1½ cups water

1½ cups low-fat milk

1 tbsp unrefined coconut oil

¼ tsp ground cinnamon

1 banana, sliced

¼ cup sliced almonds, toasted

maple syrup

salt to taste

Quinoa is the tiny grain super food from Ancient Peru. It's awesome when cooked right. It's gluten-free, high in protein, and packed with fiber, vitamins, and minerals. In this recipe, quinoa replaces oatmeal for variety. Paired with banana (the ultimate breakfast fruit), the flavors combine and really complement each other. This is a sure way to start your morning!

QUICK TIP: You will likely have to choose between white, red, or black quinoa. I recommend using white quinoa if you are not used to it, and red or black (which are a tad more rustic and earthier) if you want to try something different.

PREPARATION:

1.   Bring a heavy saucepan to medium heat. Add quinoa, water, milk, coconut oil, cinnamon, banana slices and salt to the pan. Stir well to combine.
2.   Bring the mixture to a simmer, cover and cook gently for 15 minutes. Stir from time to time.
3.   Portion into bowls. Top each bowl with a sprinkle of almonds, extra banana slices and a drizzle of maple syrup, if desired.

OPTIONS: Don't hesitate to add fruits. I often top this 'oatmeal' with fresh raspberries.

SERVING INFO: 190 calories, 0g fat, 37g carbohydrates, 1g protein, 2g fiber, 21g sugar

MARINATED FRUIT SALAD

Active time: 15 minutes (plus marinating time) | **Cook time:** N/A | **Yield:** 4 servings

INGREDIENTS:

1 cup dry white wine

¼ cup honey

1 cup pineapple, cubed

1 cup fresh strawberries, halved

½ cup kiwi

1 cup apricots or peaches, pitted and quartered

1 tbsp chopped fresh mint leaves

Really, who needs a recipe for a fruit salad? Anyone can cut a few random fruits and throw them in a bowl. While that's true, I encourage you to venture off the beaten path a bit and add some twist to an otherwise very common dish.

QUICK TIP: Yes, you can eat the skin of a kiwi, and the core of a pineapple. Maybe not as soft, sweet, and enjoyable as the actual flesh, but they are packed with tons of fiber, and worth a try.

PREPARATION:

1. Bring the wine and honey to a simmer and cook for 2 minutes. Remove from the heat.
2. Combine the fruits and mint in a large bowl. Pour the warm wine mixture over; toss to coat. Cover and refrigerate until cold, stirring occasionally, at least 2 hours.
3. Transfer the fruit mixture to a wide jar with a tight-fitting lid. Keep chilled.

10-MINUTE TIMESAVER: Don't use canned fruits to save time; they don't have the same taste and often contain added sugar. Your grocery store, however, may have some freshly cut and diced fruits, and of course you can rely on frozen fruits, especially berries.

OPTIONS: Don't hesitate to replace some fruits with others. The fruits in this recipe are easily interchangeable. If one is not available, add more of the others, or substitute with any other fresh fruit.

SERVING INFO: 330 calories, 16g fat, 4g carbohydrates, 19g protein, 1g fiber, 2g sugar

THE REAL SCRAMBLE

Active time: 15 minutes | **Cook time:** 15 minutes | **Yield:** 4 servings

INGREDIENTS:

6 large eggs

9 egg whites

⅓ cup of sundried tomatoes

3 cups of fresh spinach

2 tbsps extra-virgin olive oil

salt and pepper to taste

fresh herbs (such as parsley, chives, tarragon and chervil), finely chopped

You may think you know scrambled eggs. But you are about to discover a whole new world of flavor. The perfect scramble is a thing of beauty. It's incredibly soft, golden-colored, with rich curds that are smooth and delicious. It's more like a custard than the classic dry scramble you've had over and over.

To reach egg-liciousness, you'll need to be patient, but it'll be worth your while. It requires a little time and attention, and controlling the heat is what this game is about.

Back in my chef school days, "oeufs brouilles" (scrambled eggs), was one of the very first things we had to master. If a sixteen-year-old sous-chef can do it, you can too!

You'll need a heatproof rubber spatula and, surprise surprise, you'll have to ditch your sauté pan. Instead, use a narrow saucepan to promote even heat and to control the temperature.

QUICK TIP: Don't hesitate to change the ratio of yolks to whites. This will alter the texture but you can play with it. As a rule, egg yolks add softness to the texture, while egg whites add body.

PREPARATION:

1. Crack the eggs into a cold saucepan. Add 2 tbsps of extra-virgin olive oil to the pan. Set the pan over medium-high heat and, using a heatproof rubber spatula, mix the eggs to break them up.
2. Stir constantly, moving the pan off and on the heat so you can catch up with stirring the eggs if they are cooking too quickly.
3. Small curds with a pudding-like texture will begin to form after about 10 minutes. Pay attention to the pan, keep the curds moving and don't look away for a second. Once you've got a saucepan full of small, even but still-wet curds quickly remove the saucepan from the heat.
4. Add the salt and pepper, chopped herbs, and mix well.

APPETIZERS

SUPERCHARGED GUACAMOLE

Active time: 20 minutes | **Cook time:** none | **Yield:** 4 servings

INGREDIENTS:

4 Haas avocados, halved, seeded and peeled

2 stacks of kale

1 cup of shelled edamame

2 limes, juiced

½ red onion, diced

1 beefsteak tomato, diced

1 tbsp cilantro, chopped

2 tsps of chili oil or hot sauce

salt and pepper to taste

The world does not need another guacamole recipe. What it does need, though, is a versatile, easy-to-dip, surprisingly addictive taste, packed silly with nutritious goodness. I'm inspired by this south-of-the-border classic that includes no less than three superfoods: avocado, kale, and edamame. It looks the same as guacamole but, oh boy, the taste is wonderfully refreshing and deep. It's smooth, it's rich, it's full of fiber, and it's going to be your new favorite. Enjoy without moderation!

QUICK TIP: Choosing avocados is challenging. For guacamole, you want them soft but not too soft. The color is somewhat telling, so pay attention to the shiny, dark skin. Look for avocadoes that are plump, offer some resistance when pressing with your fingers, but still give a bit.

PREPARATION:

1. Remove the leaves of the kale from the stalk. Process them in a food processor with the edamame.
2. Add the scooped avocado pulp and lime juice. Pulse to process and transfer to a mixing bowl.
3. Add salt, chili oil or hot sauce. Then, fold in the onion, tomatoes, and cilantro into the kale-edamame mixture.
4. Let sit in the refrigerator for 1 hour and then serve.

SERVING INFO: 190 calories, 5g fat, 26g carbohydrates, 11g protein, 6g fiber, 6g sugar

TUSCAN MINESTRONE

Active time: 25 minutes | **Cook time:** 35 minutes | **Yield:** 4 servings

INGREDIENTS:

1 tbsp extra-virgin olive oil

½ cup chopped onion

½ cup chopped celery

½ cup chopped carrots

½ small can cannellini beans

½ cup shredded cabbage

½ small can diced tomatoes

1 tbsp tomato paste

3 cups low-sodium chicken broth

1 tbsp dried parsley

¼ cup whole-grain orzo pasta

2 cloves garlic, minced

¼ cup grated Parmigiano-Reggiano cheese

¼ cup fresh basil, chopped

salt and pepper to taste

Minestrone soup is always very good. What makes it exceptional is the addition of the quick pesto at the end. With it, the soup takes all its grandeur, the ingredients blend together and the taste of fresh basil and garlic fills the air.

QUICK TIP: Experiment with different vegetables. All Mediterranean vegetables (zucchini, eggplant, sweet peppers) and most legumes work very well with this easy recipe.

PREPARATION:

1. Pour extra-virgin olive oil in a heavy pot over medium-high heat.
2. Add onion, celery, and carrots. Sauté for a few minutes.
3. Add beans, cabbage, tomatoes, tomato paste, stock, parsley, salt and pepper to the pot. Bring to a simmer, cover, and cook for approximately 25 minutes until vegetables are barely tender.
4. Add pasta, and simmer for 10 minutes more. Meanwhile, mix Parmigiano-Reggiano, basil, and garlic to make a quick pesto.
5. Correct seasoning. To serve, ladle hot soup in bowls and then add the pesto.

20-MINUTE TIMESAVER: Skip the sautéing on step 1 and 2. Just add all ingredients together and bring the soup to a simmer. Resume the recipe at step 3.

OPTIONS: This awesome recipe can be made gluten-free easily by leaving out the pasta, or by using gluten-free pasta.

SERVING INFO: 150 calories, 4g fat, 26g carbohydrates, 4g protein, 6g fiber, 19g sugar

CARROT-GINGER SOUP

Active time: 15 minutes | **Cook time:** 20 minutes | **Yield:** 4 servings

INGREDIENTS:

1½ lbs. carrots, unpeeled and roughly chopped

1 onion, roughly chopped

1 tbsp fresh ginger, roughly chopped

1 garlic clove, peeled

1 tbsp extra-virgin olive oil

2 cups low-sodium chicken stock

1 cup carrot juice

1 sprig fresh tarragon leaves

1 tsp chopped chives

salt and pepper to taste

Fresh ginger really is an ingredient like no other. Its fragrance is particularly aromatic and unique. I never use dry ginger; the powder is a poor substitute and does not come close to fresh ginger. Carrot and ginger go very well together. This soup is extra delicious when made with all members of the squash family: pumpkin, butternut squash, spaghetti squash, and acorn squash, which make it a fall favorite. If you feel like it, don't hesitate to create a delightful soup tureen by carving a small pumpkin or acorn squash.

QUICK TIP: I always recommend a hand blender as the number one tool in any kitchen. It is especially useful when it comes to soup. You can process the soup to smoothness right in the pot for ultra convenience and easy cleanup.

PREPARATION:

1. Pour extra-virgin olive oil in large saucepan over medium-high heat. Add onions, fresh ginger, garlic, and salt; cook, stirring frequently, until onions are softened, about 5 minutes.

2. Increase heat to high and then add carrots, stock, carrot juice, and bring to simmer. Reduce heat to medium-low and simmer, covered, until carrots are very tender, about 20 minutes.

3. Process soup with a hand blender until smooth, 1 to 2 minutes. Season with salt and pepper to taste. Serve with a sprinkle of chives and tarragon.

20-MINUTE TIMESAVER: Skip the sautéing on step 1. Just add all ingredients together and bring the soup to a simmer. Resume the recipe on step 2.

OPTIONS: If you prefer, you can replace the carrots with most vegetables in the squash family. And if you don't have any stock on hand, use water—but the soup will have less flavor.

BROCCOLI CHEESE SOUP

Active time: 20 minutes | **Cook time:** 30 minutes | **Yield:** 4 servings

INGREDIENTS:

2 heads broccoli, cut into florets

2 tbsps extra-virgin olive oil

1 onion, diced

1 cup whole milk

1 cup chicken broth

3 tbsps coconut flour

1 cup grated Parmigiano-Reggiano

pinch of nutmeg

salt and pepper to taste

This is a really awesome way to eat your veggies! This hearty soup is perfect for winter nights: delicious, wholesome, with a nice cheesy flavor. Speaking of cheese, Parmigiano-Reggiano is packed with flavor, so you don't have to use much, and it is fairly low in fat.

QUICK TIP: Keep it rustic! Sure, you can put that soup in the blender and make it smooth, but it's best if it is chunky.

PREPARATION:

1. Preheat the oven to 375° (190°c) degrees.
2. Drizzle the broccoli with 1 tbsp of olive oil and sprinkle with salt and pepper. Place on a baking sheet cut-side down and bake until the florets begin to crisp and turn slightly brown, about 20 minutes.
3. Meanwhile, pour the remaining tbsp of olive oil in a pot over medium-high heat. Add the onions and cook until softened, 3 to 4 minutes.
4. Add coconut flour and stir. Add the milk and the stock. Add the nutmeg, then the roasted broccoli, and salt and pepper.
5. Cover the pot and simmer until the broccoli is tender, about 15 minutes. Stir in the cheese and allow it to melt.
6. Mash with a potato masher to break up the broccoli, but keep it rustic/chunky.
7. Serve hot.

15-MINUTE TIMESAVER: Skip the roasting on step 1 and 2. Just add the broccoli to the onions on step 3.

OPTIONS: This option works with broccoli, but you can substitute other green vegetables such as Brussels sprouts or leafy greens, or a combination.

FRENCH ONION SOUP

Active time: 15 minutes | **Cook time:** 50 minutes | **Yield:** 4 servings

INGREDIENTS:

2 tbsps extra-virgin olive oil

3 onions, sliced

2 garlic cloves, chopped

1 bay leaf

2 fresh thyme sprigs

1 cup red wine

3 tbsps coconut flour

1½ quart low-sodium beef broth

4 very thin slices of sprouted, one hundred percent whole-grain bread (such as Ezekiel's)

6 ounces part skim mozzarella

salt and pepper to taste

Ah, the classic French onion soup. Since I was born in France, I was pretty much born *into* it! I can't count the number of different versions I've tried, but I can guarantee you that this version will be better than any French onion soup your friends and families have ever tasted.

The problem is that French onion soup is a high-carb, high-fat calorie bomb. But not this one. Here, I'm improving it with a fat-burning nutrient ratio by replacing with higher-protein, part-skim mozzarella, over a thin slice of sprouted one hundred percent whole-grain bread, which should both take very good care of your guilt. Bon appetit!

QUICK TIP: Soups, just like casseroles and stews, are always better the next day. So I definitely recommend making this one day ahead to improve flavor, and save you time on the second day.

PREPARATION:

1. Pour the extra-virgin olive oil in a large pot over medium heat. Add the onions, garlic, bay leaves, thyme, and salt and pepper and cook until the onions are very soft and caramelized, about 25 minutes. This step is critical and you want the onions to reach a deep, rich brown color.

2. Add the wine, quickly bring to a boil, then reduce the heat and simmer until the wine has evaporated and the onions are dry, about 5 minutes.

3. Dust the onions with the flour and give them a stir. Turn the heat down to medium-low so the flour doesn't burn, and cook for 5 minutes to cook out the raw flour taste.

4. Add the beef broth, bring the soup back to a simmer, and cook for 10 minutes. Salt and pepper to taste.

5. When you're ready to serve, preheat the broiler. Meanwhile, toast the bread slices. Ladle the soup into bowls, top each with a thin slice of whole-grain bread and top with cheese. Put the bowls into the oven to melt the cheese to golden brown, about 3-5 minutes.

....

25-MINUTE TIMESAVER: Caramelizing the onions is important to give the soup its dark, rich color. But bypassing that step will save you time.

OPTIONS: This soup is also delicious without cheese, without bread, or without both! Sure, you wouldn't claim it as a French onion soup, but you'd still have a great onion soup.

CHICKEN NOODLE SOUP

Active time: 10 minutes | **Cook time:** 25 minutes | **Yield:** 4 servings

INGREDIENTS:

⅓ lb. uncooked chicken breast, chopped

½ onion, chopped

1 cup celery, chopped

1 cup carrots, washed and unpeeled, chopped

1 quart low-sodium chicken broth

½ cup whole grain pasta

2 tsps extra-virgin olive oil

1 tsp fresh basil, chopped

1 tsp fresh oregano, chopped

salt and pepper to taste

Chicken noodle soup is the ultimate comfort food, and the go-to folk remedy for colds and flu. I'm sure you have your own chicken soup memories, and probably even your own recipe. This version requires your attention, though. It only takes 10 minutes to make! And yes, it's also delicious and comforting.

QUICK TIP: To make this an ultra low-fat recipe, make it the day before. Refrigerate. Then, the next day when the soup is cold, skim the solidified fat at the top. Your broth will now be clear and fat-free.

PREPARATION:

1. Pour extra-virgin olive oil in a large pot over medium heat.
2. Sauté onion and celery in olive oil until just tender, about 5 minutes.
3. Add chicken broth and stir in chicken, carrots, basil, oregano, salt and pepper.
4. Bring to a simmer and cook for 10 minutes.
5. Add pasta and simmer for another 10 minutes.
6. Serve hot.

5-MINUTE TIMESAVER: Skip the sautéing on step 2. Just add the onions and celery to other ingredients on step 3 and resume.

OPTIONS: Add root vegetables for a variation on flavors. Some cooks also use spices such as cumin, curry and turmeric. If you are on a gluten-free diet, just replace the whole-grain pasta with whole-grain gluten-free pasta, if available.

HEALTHY CAESAR SALAD

Active time: 5 minutes | **Cook time:** none | **Yield:** 1⅓ cup

INGREDIENTS:

2 heads of romaine lettuce

2 tbsps extra-virgin olive oil

2 small garlic cloves, minced

1 tsp anchovy paste

1 tbsp freshly squeezed lemon juice

1 tsp Dijon mustard

1 tsp Worcestershire sauce

1 cup plain Greek yogurt

¼ cup freshly grated Parmigiano-Reggiano

¼ cup of whole-grain, unsweetened cereals (such as Ezekiel's)

salt and pepper to taste

Did you know the Caesar salad (the most famous salad in America) was likely born south of the border, in Mexico? My version is a fantastic, lighter twist on the classic. To take it a step further, how about using kale instead of romaine? It's also more than a salad! Try the dressing as a dip!

QUICK TIP: Give anchovy a chance! Anchovy paste is most likely available in your grocery store. If not, just use canned anchovies and grind them quickly with a fork.

PREPARATION:

1. In a medium bowl, whisk together the garlic, anchovy paste, lemon juice, olive oil, Dijon mustard and Worcestershire sauce. Add the Greek yogurt, half of the Parmigiano-Reggiano, salt and pepper and whisk until well combined. Taste and adjust to your liking.
2. Wash, dry, and cut the romaine lettuce. In a stainless steel bowl, toss with the dressing. Transfer to a salad bowl.
3. Sprinkle with the remaining Parmigiano-Reggiano and the cereals. Serve at once.

5-MINUTE TIMESAVER: A food processor would blend ingredients into a heavenly smooth dressing, and save you precious time. Also, conveniently, this Caesar dressing can be made ahead. The best way is to refrigerate it in a squeeze bottle.

OPTIONS: Don't let the classic recipe control your creativity; many options are available. Replacing romaine lettuce with kale or other greens is a healthy possibility. Feel free to add ingredients too. Try cherry tomatoes, cooked green beans or asparagus, or leftover Brussels sprouts from page 201. Add protein such as cooked shrimp or scallops, grilled chicken, grilled steak or salmon.

★ FAV ★

SERVING INFO: 370 calories, 29g fat, 15g carbohydrates, 12g protein, 4g fiber, 10g sugar

CAPRESE SALAD WITH BURRATA

Active time: 20 minutes | **Cook time:** none | **Yield:** 4 servings

INGREDIENTS:

For the dressing:

½ cup cherry tomatoes

4 tbsps extra-virgin olive oil

2 tbsps of vinegar (balsamic or sherry are best)

1 clove garlic, minced

1 tsp Dijon mustard

1 tsp fresh basil

salt and pepper to taste

For the salad:

6 large beefsteak tomatoes

1 cup cherry tomatoes, halved

1 8-ounce balls burrata mozzarella, torn into quarters

½ cup of loosely packed basil, torn

2 tbsps sliced chives

salt and pepper to taste

You know real mozzarella cheese. Not shredded, but the real balls of soft Italian mozzarella di buffala, which are usually kept in brine. It's nutritious and tastes great. Let me introduce you to mozza's cousin, burrata. It closely resembles a ball of mozzarella, but when split open, it's filled with a rich tasty filling of mozzarella pieces and cream. It's delicious but we're not using much, as this recipe is all about tomato and basil!

QUICK TIP: Mozzarella di buffala is good. Burrata is great. But if you can put your hands on smoked mozzarella, then you're in luck, my friend. That would add a serious dimension to any dish you use it with, including this one.

PREPARATION:

1. Make the dressing. In a food processor, combine the tomatoes, olive oil, vinegar, garlic, Dijon mustard, fresh basil, salt and pepper.
2. Using a serrated knife, slice the beefsteak tomatoes in rounds, and the cherry tomatoes in half.
3. Transfer the tomatoes to a large, wide platter, and drizzle with the dressing. Slice the burrata and place around the tomatoes. Scatter the herbs on top of the tomatoes and burrata.
4. Finish the salad with another drizzle of olive oil and a sprinkle of salt.
5. Serve immediately.

5-MINUTE TIMESAVER: Use your premade vinaigrette recipe from page 87.

OPTIONS: Of course, burrata can be replaced by part-skim mozzarella for a slightly better nutritional option.

ROQUEFORT, PEACH, AND ALMOND SALAD

Active time: 15 minutes | **Cook time:** 10 minutes | **Yield:** 4 servings

INGREDIENTS:

1 head of Bibb lettuce, torn into bite-size pieces

2 peaches, peeled, cored and quartered

1 ounce Roquefort cheese, crumbled

¼ cup almonds

¼ cup extra-virgin olive oil

2 tbsps red wine vinegar

1 tsp Dijon mustard

salt and pepper to taste

The more I cook, the more I'm convinced that the variety of tastes and textures play a huge role in our appreciation of food. Winning combinations often involve something tangy, something sweet, and something crunchy. Salads benefit from a classic cheese-fruit-nut pairing. Thats why this salad is a real winner.

QUICK TIP: Use a vegetable peeler to peel the peaches if they are barely ripe or use a knife if they are very ripe.

PREPARATION:

1. Place the almonds on a baking sheet and toast for 10 minutes in a 350° (180°c) oven.
2. For the dressing, blend oil, vinegar, mustard, salt, and pepper.
3. In a large serving bowl, layer lettuce, peaches, and blue cheese. Toss with dressing.
4. Sprinkle with almonds, and serve.

5-MINUTE TIME SAVER: Use your premade vinaigrette recipe from page 87 and skip step 2.

OPTIONS: Bibb lettuce, almonds, and blue cheese are an important trio. But you can use any lettuce, any nut, and any cheese to create a winning combination.

SPINACH, ROASTED FENNEL AND GRAPEFRUIT SALAD

Active time: 15 minutes | **Cook time:** 30 minutes | **Yield:** 4 servings

INGREDIENTS:

1 fennel bulb, halved lengthwise, core removed, then sliced lengthwise ½-inch thick

3 tbsps extra-virgin olive oil, divided

2 red grapefruits

2 cups of baby spinach

½ cup pitted cured black olives

salt and pepper to taste

Eat as much as you want! This salad is packed with aromatic flavors, unique complexity, excellent nutrition, and is ridiculously low in fat and carbohydrates. Roasting fennel concentrates its flavor, making it sweet, tender, and slightly crisp around the edges. That chewy goodness is then tossed with spinach, grapefruit segments, and briny-cured olives. The result is a slightly warm salad that has a complex range of flavors and textures.

PREPARATION:

1. Preheat oven to 350° (180°c). Line a rimmed baking sheet with foil.
2. Toss the fennel wedges with 1 tbsp of the olive oil. Season with salt and pepper and roast until tender and the edges are browned and crispy, about 30 minutes.
3. Meanwhile, using a Microplane grater, grate the zest of the grapefruit into a bowl. Using a sharp knife, cut the grapefruit in half crosswise. With a tsp, remove the pulp between each segment. Squeeze the juice and reserve.
4. In a large salad bowl, combine the spinach, olives, grapefruit segments (reserving the juice for later).
5. As soon as the fennel is done roasting, add it to the bowl along with 2 tbsps of the reserved grapefruit juice and the remaining olive oil. Season with salt and pepper if needed, and toss to combine. Serve at once.

35-MINUTE TIMESAVER: Fennel is also excellent uncooked. You can skip steps 1 and 2 and start the recipe on step 3.

OPTIONS: Sure, you can replace the aromatic fennel by something equally crunchy like celery. Grapefruit may be switched with oranges, and spinach can be replaced by any greens such as arugula or kale.

FAV

SERVING INFO: 240 calories, 0g fat, 49g carbohydrates, 19g protein, 16g fiber, 2g sugar

MEXICAN THREE BEAN SALAD

Active time: 15 minutes | **Cook time:** N/A | **Yield:** 4 servings

INGREDIENTS:

1 small can black beans, rinsed and drained

1 small can kidney beans, rinsed and drained

1 cup shelled frozen edamame beans

½ red bell pepper, chopped

½ red onion, chopped

2 tbsps extra-virgin olive oil

2 tsps fresh lime juice

a dash of hot pepper sauce

1 clove of garlic, minced

2 cups of fresh cilantro, chopped

salt and pepper to taste

Beans are about protein, fiber, and overall awesome nutrition. Besides that, what I love about them is they are filling. Stuff your face and stay fit; that's what it's all about!

QUICK TIP: If you own a slow cooker, there is an easy way to cook dry beans and skip the canned variety. Just place any dry beans (not lentils) in a slow cooker with enough water (2 inches above beans), aromatics (bay leaves, onions, garlic, etc...), and optional protein. Cook on low for 6 to 8 hours.

PREPARATION:

1. In a large bowl, combine beans, bell peppers, and red onion.
2. In a small bowl, whisk together olive oil, lime juice, salt, garlic, cilantro, salt and pepper. Season to taste with hot sauce.
3. Pour olive oil dressing over vegetables; mix well. Chill and serve.

5-MINUTE TIMESAVER: Use your premade vinaigrette recipe from page 87, add chopped cilantro and hot sauce, and skip step 2.

OPTIONS: Experiment with beans. Navy, garbanzo, cannellini, pinto, and even cooked lentils all work very well.

GRILLED CORN & SUMMER VEGETABLE SALAD

Active time: 30 minutes | **Cook time:** 10 minutes | **Yield:** 4 servings

INGREDIENTS:

2 ears of yellow corn, husked

1 poblano pepper

¼ of a red onion, very thinly sliced

juice and zest of 2 lemons

2 small zucchini, halved lengthwise and into half rounds

½ cup walnuts, toasted

⅓ cup Italian parsley, roughly chopped

⅓ cup mint, roughly chopped

⅛ cup finely chopped chives

¼ cup extra-virgin olive oil

1 tbsp sherry vinegar

1 tbsp flax seeds

1 cup of feta, crumbled

salt and pepper to taste

Giving you options while making recipes is important to me. Here, I urge you to make this recipe as-is. It is truly wonderful and my wife Carissa's favorite. The pairing of poblano pepper, grilled corn and raw zucchini is a match made in heaven, and the fresh herbs and light feta cheese top it off with brio.

QUICK TIP: To toast the walnuts, or any nuts for that matter, simply put them raw on a baking sheet, arranging them quickly in one layer. Bake in a preheated oven around 350F (180C) for about 10 minutes. You'll start smelling them as they fill the air with irresistible scents.

PREPARATION:

1. Bring your grill up to medium-high heat
2. Place the corn and pepper on the grill and cook, turning often, until tender and charred in spots, 10 to 12 minutes.
3. Transfer the corn and peppers to a clean cutting board. Put the pepper into a re-sealable plastic bag. You should be able to remove the skin easily. Remove the kernels from the cobs and place in a large bowl. Remove the stems and seeds from the pepper and roughly chop and add to corn. Add the onion, zucchini, walnuts, parsley, mint, chives, olive oil, vinegar, and flax seeds and toss to combine. Season with salt and pepper.
4. Top with the feta and serve.

15-MINUTE TIMESAVER: I don't recommend skipping the grilling part and using canned or frozen corn. It is a possibility if you're in a rush, though. In that case, start the recipe at step 3.

OPTIONS: You could use cucumber instead of raw zucchini, if you prefer.

CAULIFLOWER TABOULEH

Active time: 20 minutes | **Cook time:** none | **Yield:** 4 servings

INGREDIENTS:

⅔ head cauliflower, cut into florets

½ cup of couscous

2 tbsps dried cranberries

1 large tomato, diced

2 scallions, sliced

1 cup Italian parsley

½ cup mint

1 tbsp of flax seeds

1 tbsp of toasted sesame seeds

2 tbsps of pistachio, toasted

2 tbsps extra-virgin olive oil

zest and juice from 2 lemons

salt and pepper to taste

I remember my summers in the South of France, when as a kid we would dive into the cobalt blue Mediterranean Sea, swim for hours, and come back for a mid-afternoon al fresco lunch, which often included Tabouleh. It was my mom's idea of fast food.

Tabouleh is a world-renowned Mediterranean salad, traditionally made of couscous, tomatoes, chopped parsley and mint, and perfectly seasoned with extra-virgin olive oil, lemon juice, and salt.

While the traditional recipe is already a healthy option, here is my version, packed with more vitamin C, potassium, and fiber. I simply replace most of the couscous with finely chopped raw cauliflower, which still tastes and feels surprisingly similar. It is delicious and extremely nutritious, while helping you cut carbs for faster fat loss.

QUICK TIP: This is a no-cook recipe. The couscous becomes tender, over time, by absorbing the lemon juice, extra-virgin olive oil, and the natural juice of the tomatoes.

PREPARATION:

1. In a small container, combine the cranberries and the couscous with ⅓ cup of lukewarm water, and allow it to reconstitute, about 20 minutes.
2. Working in batches, pulse the cauliflower in a food processor until it has broken down into crumbles the size of dry couscous.
3. Reserve the cauliflower, and use the food processor to chop scallions, parsley, and mint.
4. Transfer the cauliflower, herbs, couscous and cranberries to a large mixing bowl along with the tomatoes, flax and sesame seeds, olive oil and lemon zest and juice. Season generously with salt and toss.
5. Allow to rest, preferably overnight or at least 1 hour.

★ FAV ★

TIMESAVER: You can finely chop raw cauliflower by hand as I did as a sous-chef in France, but using a food processor works really well for this and cuts down your time in the kitchen. Roughly cut cauliflower chunks and then pulse in the food processor until you get really tiny, even bits. Same with all herbs.

OPTIONS:
1. The balance of couscous vs. cauliflower is up to you! If cauliflower is not something you love, make this recipe using couscous only. If you eat gluten-free, or simply want to pack on fiber, omit the couscous and make it one hundred percent cauliflower.
2. Add nuts, seeds, dried fruits or fresh herbs for even more nutrients.

SERVING INFO: 260 calories, 11g fat, 35g carbohydrate, 8g protein, 7g fiber, 8g sugar

SERVING INFO: 150 calories, 10g fat, 12g carbohydrates, 2g protein, 4g fiber, 8g sugar

WALDORF SALAD

Active time: 15 minutes | **Cook time:** none | **Yield:** 4 servings

INGREDIENTS:

8 celery stalks, thinly sliced on a bias

⅓ cup raw walnuts

1 red apple, cored, quartered, skin on

2 tbsps roughly chopped yellow celery leaves

2 tbsps plain Greek yogurt

1 tbsp freshly squeezed lemon juice

1 tbsp extra-virgin olive oil

salt and pepper to taste

The history of the Waldorf salad dates back to 1896. Celery, apple, and walnut. Hardly anything new until today! It was time to revamp this great classic, toss the mayonnaise, and replace it with a more nutritious Greek yogurt. You see, plain Greek yogurt is packed with protein, calcium, and is low in carbohydrates. There is something so gratifying about crunchy ingredients. And crunch is what this salad is all about. Imagine this: celery, apple, and walnut. Nothing gets crunchier than that.

QUICK TIP: Toasting walnuts really increases their crunch. Don't skip that step.

PREPARATION:

1. Preheat the oven to 350° (180°c). Spread the walnuts on a baking sheet and toast in the oven until golden brown, about 8 minutes.
2. Meanwhile, make the dressing by mixing yogurt, lemon juice, extra-virgin olive oil, and salt and pepper.
3. Dice the apples.
4. Place celery and leaves in a medium bowl. Add the walnuts, the diced apples, as well as the dressing. Mix well.
5. Refrigerate until serving time.

10-MINUTE TIMESAVER: Toasting walnuts really is a good idea for increased taste and texture. However, skipping step 1 will save you 10 minutes.

OPTIONS: Add variety by replacing walnuts with cashew or Brazil.

SERVING INFO: 280 calories, 8g fat, 66g carbohydrates, 18g protein, 9g fiber, 10g sugar

OVERNIGHT SAVORY OATMEAL

Active time: Less than 5 minutes | **Cook time:** none | **Yield:** 4 servings

INGREDIENTS:

2 cups steel cut
rolled oats

2 cups low-fat milk

4 tbsps plain
Greek yogurt

1 tsp maple syrup

1 tsp fresh oregano

1 tsp curry powder

1 tbsp toasted
pistachios

2 tbsps dried
cranberries

½ tsp cayenne pepper

salt and pepper
to taste

So here is the concept. Follow me on this one. One night before bed, you mix oatmeal with whatever ingredients strike your fancy. You put it in a bowl in your refrigerator. Entire prep time is less than 5 minutes. No cooking. You go to bed. The next day, you come back to your refrigerator, open the door, and there is your lunch.

QUICK TIP: Don't hesitate to change ingredients, as long as you respect the ratio of I volume of oats to I volume of milk. Leftover protein from last night's dinner works well. The world is your oatmeal.

PREPARATION:

1. Mix together all ingredients, cover, and refrigerate overnight.

TIMESAVER: Are you kidding me?

SOUTHWESTERN EGG ROLLS

Active time: 20 minutes | **Cook time:** 15 minutes | **Yield:** 4 servings

INGREDIENTS:

2 tbsps extra-virgin olive oil

1 skinless, boneless chicken breast

2 tbsps scallions, minced

2 tbsps red bell pepper, minced

⅓ cup frozen corn kernels

¼ cup black beans, rinsed and drained

2 tbsps frozen chopped spinach, thawed and drained

2 tbsps jalapeno peppers, minced

½ tbsp Italian parsley, minced

½ tsp ground cumin

½ tsp chili powder

¼ cup shredded Monterey Jack cheese

4 taco-size sprouted whole-grain tortillas (such as Ezekiel 4:9)

salt and pepper to taste

These aren't traditional egg rolls! Small flour tortillas are stuffed with an exciting blend of Southwestern-style ingredients, then deep fried until golden brown.

PREPARATION:

1. Preheat oven at 375˚ (190˚c).
2. Rub 1 tbsp olive oil over chicken breast. In a medium pan over medium heat, cook chicken approximately 5 minutes per side, until meat is no longer pink and juices run clear. Remove the chicken from the pan and set aside.
3. In the same pan, stir in scallions and red pepper. Cook and stir 5 minutes, until tender.
4. Dice chicken and mix into the pan with onion and red pepper. Mix in corn, black beans, spinach, jalapeno peppers, parsley, cumin, chili powder, salt and pepper. Cook and stir 5 minutes, until well blended and tender. Remove from heat and stir in Monterey Jack cheese so that it melts.
5. Wrap tortillas with a clean, lightly moist cloth. Microwave on high approximately 1 minute, or until hot and pliable.
6. Spoon even amounts of the mixture into each tortilla. Fold ends of tortillas, then roll tightly around mixture. Secure with toothpicks. Brush lightly to coat with remaining olive oil. Arrange in an oven-proof dish.
7. Bake in the oven until golden and crisp, about 15 minutes.

12-MINUTE TIME SAVER: Use leftover cooked chicken on pages 95 or 97 and skip step 1.

HEALTHY CHICKEN WINGS

Active time: 25 minutes | **Cook time:** 25 minutes | **Yield:** 4 servings

INGREDIENTS:

20 chicken drumettes

3 tbsps Sriracha sauce
(or hot sauce)

3 tbsps minced garlic

2 tbsps Italian parsley,
minced

2 tsps of dried oregano

⅓ cup blue cheese,
crumbled

1 cup plain
Greek yogurt

4 stalks of celery

salt and pepper
to taste

Are you ready for Monday Night Football? Chicken wings are your companion and mine for the night. I twisted this classic for you, just enough to end up with taste and convenience, without the fat. First, chicken drumsticks offer more meat and less fat than wings, so I recommend choosing them. I also ditched the standard deep-frying in favor of a two-step steam-and-roast method. What's the difference? Not much in terms of taste and texture. The wings are still plump and juicy, and slightly spicy. But my method seriously cuts down on the fat content, so you can eat more without worrying.

PREPARATION:

1. Preheat oven at 425° (220°c). Add one inch of water to a saucepan and bring to a simmer. Place chicken in the saucepan. Steam, covered, for 10 minutes. Remove chicken from saucepan; cool. Pat dry.

2. Remove skin on the chicken drumsticks.

3. Toss with Sriracha sauce, garlic, Italian parsley, oregano, and a pinch of salt. Lay on a baking sheet in one layer. Bake in oven for 15 minutes.

4. Meanwhile, mix the yogurt with the blue cheese. Add salt and pepper to taste. Cut the celery stalks into 3- to 4-inch long pieces.

5. To serve, put the blue cheese dip in a bowl, and display it on a large round tray. Place the chicken drumsticks and celery on the platter around the dip.

SERVING INFO: 240 calories, 16g fat, 13g carbohydrates, 10g protein, 3g fiber, 2g sugar

SKINNY PIGS IN A BLANKET

Active time: 20 minutes | **Cook time:** 30 minutes | **Yield:** 96 pigs in a blanket

INGREDIENTS:

16 uncured, organic beef hot dogs

¾ cup coconut flour

1½ cups whole grain flour

1 cup almond flour

3 tsps baking powder

1 tsp sea salt

1 cup melted butter

1 cup plain Greek yogurt

¼ cup Dijon mustard

This recipe was the toughest, most difficult to hack. Here's the secret... First, let's make sure we only use organic beef hot dogs (which by definition do not contain antibiotics and hormones). They're also low in sodium, and free of nitrate (uncured). Second, let's reduce the fat (usually butter or worse) and replace most of it with a healthy Greek yogurt. Last but not least, I chose a combination of high-fiber, low-GI, high-protein flours which give us just the right amount of great taste. And the benefit of wholesomeness. Finally enjoy the little buggers without guilt!

PREPARATION:

1. Mix flours, baking powder, salt, butter and yogurt together. Knead ingredients together in a bowl for 2 or 3 minutes.
2. Using a rolling pin, roll the dough to a ⅛inch thickness. Brush Dijon mustard onto the rolled-out dough. Use a knife to cut the dough into 1 inch x 1 inch squares.
3. Cut each wiener in 6 and place one piece on each rectangle.
4. Roll each rectangle of dough onto the wiener, and place it on a well-greased baking dish. Bake at 350° (180°c) for 30 minutes or until the crust is lightly browned.

TIMESAVER: You can freeze the pigs in a blanket. They can then be baked straight from frozen, which saves a ton of time.

BASIC VINAIGRETTE

Active time: Under 5 minutes | **Cook time:** none | **Yield:** ½ cup

INGREDIENTS:

6 tbsps extra-virgin olive oil

2 tbsps of vinegar

1 clove garlic, minced

1 tsp Dijon mustard

1 tsp fresh herbs

salt to taste

ground black pepper

Have you ever read the ingredients on the back label of a processed salad dressing?

The truth is that you can make phenomenal salad dressings at home with very little effort. This recipe is the base. You start with the base and then add on. Experiment with different vinegars: balsamic, sherry, white or red wine, Champagne, apple cider, or even a vinegar glaze. Add any fresh herbs, Greek yogurt, shallots, caramelized onions, bee pollen, lemon juice, any citrus juice or zest. The possibilities are endless.

Don't compromise on olive oil, though. Sure, you can make good vinaigrette with canola, vegetable or any basic extra-virgin olive oil. But using the best extra-virgin your money can buy is the way to go. Only then will your salad dressing become a natural salad-enhancer, and take a simple iceberg lettuce to greatness. Don't use *pure* olive oil. Walnut or grape seed oil works well too.

QUICK TIP: This salad dressing is not meant to be emulsified, but you can use a hand blender to bind ingredients together and thicken the dressing. Mustard is a natural emulsifier and will do a fantastic job.

PREPARATION:
1. Combine the garlic, mustard, vinegar, salt, pepper, and extra-virgin olive oil in a container or glass jar with a lid.
2. Shake vigorously until the oil and vinegar are well emulsified.
3. Serve with your favorite greens

TIMESAVER: Make large quantities of vinaigrette (say 1 or 2 quarts at a time) and refrigerate it in a bottle or jar, or better yet, a squeeze bottle. It will be ready when you need it.

OPTIONS: I really encourage you to be creative with this salad dressing. Keep the 2:1 oil-vinegar ratio as a foundation. Then play with various oils and vinegar to develop your own creative flavors.

FAT-BURNING SALAD DRESSING

Active time: Under 5 minutes | **Cook time:** N/A | **Yield:** ½ cup

INGREDIENTS:

3 tbsps extra-virgin olive oil

3 tbsps freshly squeezed lemon juice

⅓ cup apple cider vinegar

salt and pepper to taste

Get the biggest bowl you own. Fill it with salad greens, add other vegetables, an optional carbohydrate source (such as berries, chickpeas, or quinoa), pile it up with lean protein, and an optional healthy fat source like organic eggs, cheese, or avocado. Now, toss your salad with this slightly acidic dressing and experience great food while stimulating fat burning and feeling full.

TIMESAVER: Make large quantities of this dressing (say 1 or 2 quarts at a time) and refrigerate it in a bottle or jar, or better yet, a squeeze bottle. It will be ready when you need it.

OPTIONS: Keep the same ingredients and add fresh herbs such as chopped cilantro, mint, parsley, basil or tarragon. This will enhance flavors and add nutrients.

MAIN COURSES

BOURBON CHICKEN

Active time: 15 minutes | **Cook time:** 20 minutes | **Yield:** 4 servings

INGREDIENTS:

2 lbs. boneless chicken breasts, cut into bite-size pieces

1 tbsps extra-virgin olive oil

1 garlic clove, minced

1 tsp ginger, minced

¾ tsp crushed red pepper flakes

¼ cup apple juice

3 tbsps honey

2 tbsps tomato paste

1 tbsps cider vinegar

4 tbsps (gluten-free) soy sauce

Bourbon Chicken is a classic in Cajun or Chinese fast casual restaurants alike. Chances are you've tasted a sample at the mall. Not easy to hack, right? The original recipe was dark and sugary, and loaded with cornstarch. I cut the sweets to a minimum. This recipe is so good my children gobble it up in no time.

QUICK TIP: This dish will be even better the next day. So refrigerate, let the flavors mingle overnight, and serve the following day.

PREPARATION:

1. Heat oil in a large skillet over medium-high heat. Sear chicken until lightly browned. Do not overcrowd the pan. You may want to do 2 batches. Set aside when done.
2. Add remaining ingredients; mix well and bring to a simmer.
3. Reduce heat and simmer for 15 minutes. Serve hot.

10-MINUTE TIMESAVER: If you buy chicken tenders, you won't need to cut the chicken into bite-size pieces. That will save you about 10 minutes.

FAMILY CHICKEN NUGGETS

Active time: 15 minutes | **Cook time:** 10 minutes | **Yield:** 4 servings

INGREDIENTS:

2 lbs. chicken tenders

1 cup coconut flour

2 tsps baking powder

1 egg

2 egg whites

1 cup unsweetened, whole-grain cereals (such as Ezekiel or Bob's Red Mill brand), processed into crumbs

½ tsp of cayenne pepper

1 tsp of paprika

salt and pepper to taste

You can give your kids what they want. They just don't have to know that we tweaked it—for their own good, of course! The most difficult dishes to adapt to a good and healthy lifestyle are those involving deep frying and breading. I definitely recommend skipping the deep-frying and choosing a roasting technique. Sure, you lose a bit of crunch, but you also eliminate a lot of fat. For the breading, I recommend using an unsweetened, whole-grain cereal such as those produced by Ezekiel or Bob's Red Mill. Both brands carry nutritious and wholesome cereals without the sugar and high fructose corn syrup contained in almost every other maker. Pulse the flakes in a food processor until they turn into crumbs.

QUICK TIP: I do my best to drastically cut down the fat in all of my recipes. Having said that, a cooking spray is a good tool to add a minimal amount of fat on the outside of the chicken. Watch the nuggets turn a beautiful golden brown color, very close to the appearance of deep-frying. Simply spray the outside of the chicken nuggets before roasting them in the oven.

PREPARATION:

1. Preheat oven to 400° (200°c) degrees. Brush 1 baking sheet with a bit of extra-virgin olive oil.
2. Prepare a 'breading' section. In a small bowl, stir together the flour, baking powder, cayenne pepper, paprika, and a pinch of salt. In a second bowl, beat the eggs until they are blended together. Place the "breadcrumbs" in a third bowl.
3. Dip the chicken strips into the flour mixture until they are all coated. One at a time, dunk strips in the egg mixture. Transfer to the third bowl, and scoop the crumbs up over the strips to coat. Repeat with remaining chicken tenders. Evenly lay them on the baking sheet.
4. Bake until outside is crispy and inside is soft, about 10 minutes.

5-MINUTE TIMESAVER: Instead of using bowls for the breading section, use resealable plastic bags. Less messy and the clean up will be a breeze.

OPTIONS: For a gluten-free diet, use gluten-free breadcrumbs.

HOMEMADE ROTISSERIE CHICKEN

Active time: 20 minutes | **Cook time:** 1 hour | **Yield:** 4 servings

INGREDIENTS:

1 large chicken, patted dry

2 thyme sprigs

2 cloves of garlic, minced

1 lemon

1 tbsp extra-virgin olive oil

salt and pepper, to taste

Why buy an overpriced rotisserie chicken when you can make your own in little time, while controlling the ingredients? Rotisserie chicken is easy. All you have to do is put the bird on a pan and place it in the oven with a few seasonings. Feel free to be creative! As long as you have a chicken, some salt and pepper, and a little extra-virgin olive oil to trigger a nice, golden crust, you're in good shape. The rest is up to you. Sprinkle some lemon pepper, oregano, fresh ginger or other herb and rub it into the bird. It really is that easy.

QUICK TIP: Resting, resting, resting. It's my number one tip when roasting meat. Once the chicken is fully cooked, make sure that you rest it for at least 10-20 minutes. That will rehydrate the bird with its own juices and make the meat tender and full of flavor.

PREPARATION:

1. Grate the skin of the lemon, and squeeze its juice.
2. Preheat the oven to 400° (200°c). Place the whole chicken into a roasting pan. Rub the thyme, garlic, and grated lemon on the skin. Season with salt and pepper. Rub 1 tbsp of the olive oil and the lemon juice all over the body of the chicken. Using kitchen twine, tie the legs together.
3. Place the pan in the oven and roast until the chicken begins to turn golden-brown, about 30 minutes.
4. At that point lower the heat to 350° (180°c) and roast for another 30 minutes, until the bird is golden-brown all over and the skin is crisp. The chicken is done when the juices run clear from the thigh. Transfer the chicken to a cutting board and allow to rest for 10 minutes before carving.

SERVING INFO: 440 calories, 33g fat, 20g carbohydrates, 27g protein, 13g fiber, 7 net carbs

CHICKEN POT PIE

Active time: 20 minutes | **Cook time:** 35 minutes | **Yield:** 1 9-inch pie

INGREDIENTS:

For the chicken:

1 lb. skinless, boneless chicken breast halves, roughly diced

1 cup carrots, unpeeled, washed, and sliced

1 cup frozen green peas

½ cup celery, sliced

3 tbsps extra-virgin olive oil

⅓ cup onion, chopped

4 tbsps coconut flour

2 tbsps buckwheat flour

2 cups chicken broth

½ cup low-fat milk

salt and pepper to taste

For the crust:

¾ cup coconut flour

1½ cup whole grain flour

1 cup almond flour

3 teaspoons baking powder

1 tsp sea salt

1 cup melted butter

1 cup plain Greek yogurt

Is there a more traditional, comfort dish than chicken pot pie? But, how do you also make it fat-burning? Let's just pack the classic with chicken, vegetables, and use a smart combo of buckwheat and coconut flours (I call them "superflours") to get us where we want to be.

PREPARATION:

1. Preheat oven to 400° (200°c.)
2. In a large saucepan over medium heat, cook onions in olive oil until soft and translucent. Stir in flours, salt and pepper. Slowly stir in chicken broth and milk. Simmer over medium-low heat until it thickens a bit.
3. Add chicken, carrots, peas, and celery. Simmer for 10 minutes, covered. Remove from heat and set aside.
4. Place the chicken mixture in the bottom of a pie mold. Make the crust: In a stainless steel bowl, mix all ingredients together and knead for 5 minutes. Rest for 10 minutes, then roll out until it reaches a thickness of ¼ inch.
5. Cover top of the pie mold with crust, seal edges, and cut away excess dough.
6. Bake in the preheated oven for 30 minutes, or until pastry is golden brown and filling is bubbly. Cool for 10 minutes before serving.

15-MINUTE TIMESAVER: I make my pie crust in big batches, section them into 10-inch balls, and freeze them in resealable plastic bags. That way, I always have some ready-made pie crust on hand.

otein, 4g fibe

CHICKEN CORDON BLEU

Active time: 15 minutes | **Cook time:** 20 minutes | **Yield:** 4 servings

INGREDIENTS:

4 skinless, boneless chicken breasts

4 slices Swiss cheese

4 slices ham

6 tbsps coconut flour

1 tsp paprika

a pinch of cayenne pepper

3 tbsps extra-virgin olive oil

½ cup dry white wine

½ cup chicken stock

salt and pepper to taste

'Cordon Bleu' is a French term, literally translated as 'blue ribbon,' which originally referred to an award for culinary excellence given to cooks. The dish Chicken Cordon Bleu is made with chicken, ham, and cheese.

QUICK TIP: Pounding the chicken breast makes it tender and easy to chew. It also allows the sauce to *penetrate* into the meat, resulting in a flavorful chicken and sauce.

PREPARATION:

1. Pound chicken breasts between two layers of plastic film. Place a cheese and ham slice on each breast within ½ inch of the edges. Fold the edges of the chicken over the filling,mand secure with toothpicks. Sprinkle with salt and pepper to taste.

2. Mix the flour, paprika, and cayenne in a small bowl, and coat the chicken pieces.

3. Heat the olive oil in a large skillet over medium-high heat, and cook chicken until browned on all sides. Add the wine and stock. Reduce heat to low, cover, and simmer for 15 minutes, until chicken is no longer pink and juices run clear.

4. Remove the toothpicks, and transfer the breasts to a warm platter.

5. Boil the sauce to reduce it, stirring until slightly thickened, and pour over the chicken.

6. Serve warm.

CHICKEN PICCATA

Active time: 15 minutes | **Cook time:** 25 minutes | **Yield:** 4 servings

INGREDIENTS:

4 chicken breasts, skinless and boneless, cut in half crosswise

4 tbsps coconut flour

1 tsp paprika

a pinch of cayenne pepper

4 tbsps extra-virgin olive oil

½ cup dry white wine

⅓ cup fresh lemon juice

½ cup low-sodium chicken stock

¼ cup brined capers, rinsed

½ onion, minced or thinly diced

⅓ cup fresh Italian parsley, chopped

salt and pepper to taste

Chicken Piccata is a famous dish, Italian in origin, though many people don't know this. In Italy, the recipe is made with veal. The quick sauce contains capers, wine, lemon, and Italian parsley. It is usually finished with chunks of butter but we'll leave that part out for obvious reasons. Chicken Piccata is often my go-to dinner. It's a one-pot meal and it's superfast to make.

PREPARATION:

1. Pound chicken breast pieces between 2 layers of plastic film, so it tenderizes and size is uniform. Season with salt and pepper.
2. Mix flour, paprika, and cayenne. Dredge chicken in flour and shake off excess.
3. In a large skillet over medium high heat, heat up olive oil. Sear chicken in a hot pan, a few pieces at a times, and cook for a couple of minutes. When chicken is browned, flip and cook other side for another couple of minutes. Remove and set aside.
4. Into the same pan over high heat, add the capers and onions and sauté for a minute. Then add the wine, then the lemon juice and stock. Bring to boil, scraping up brown bits from the pan for extra flavor.
5. Return all the chicken to the pan and simmer for 5 minutes. Move chicken from pan to serving platter. Boil to reduce sauce by half. Pour sauce over chicken and garnish with parsley.

OPTIONS: Options are plentiful. Feel free to add diced tomatoes and play with fresh herbs, such as tarragon or chive. Sprinkle with pine nuts or toasted macadamia nuts for a creative twist

CHICKEN TIKKA MASALA

Active time: 20 minutes (plus marinating time) | **Cook time:** 20 minutes | **Yield:** 4 servings

INGREDIENTS:

2 lbs. skinless, boneless chicken breasts, cut into strips

6 garlic cloves, finely grated

4 tsps finely grated peeled ginger

2 tsps ground curry

4 tsps garam masala

2 tsps ground cumin

½ tsp Cayenne pepper

1½ cups plain Greek yogurt

3 tbsps extra-virgin olive oil

1 small onion, thinly sliced

¼ cup tomato paste

6 cardamom pods, crushed

1 small can diced tomatoes

1 cup coconut milk

¾ cup chopped fresh cilantro

salt to taste

I've never been to India, but I lived in Oxford, England, where the Indian community is active and lively. Indian restaurants there are plentiful, and the quality of the cuisine is unparalleled. You can walk up to any Indian restaurant in England and be welcomed with the very best of Indian cuisine. Chicken Tikka Masala is now known all over the world, and that's a good thing. The dish is marinated in a spice and yogurt sauce. The yogurt helps tenderize the meat. Garlic, ginger, curry and other spices blend overnight to add deep flavors, without being too spicy. Usually Tikka Masala is roasted in a Tandoor oven, a high-temp clay oven that 'broils' the meat. This recipe is adapted to your home kitchen, yet reveals the true taste of India.

QUICK TIP: Like many sauce dishes, Chicken Tikka Masala is even better the day after you prepare it. Why? It's a basic principle of chemistry called osmosis and diffusion. Every time a dish is started at cold temperature, and brought back to a hot temperature, there is a great exchange of flavors. That happens when you cook your Tikka Masala. If you chill it after cooking, then reheat it the next day, you again start that osmosis and diffusion process, and enhance the flavors.

PREPARATION:

1. Combine garlic, ginger, cayenne pepper, curry, garam masala, and cumin in a small bowl.
2. Whisk yogurt, salt, and half of spice mixture in a medium bowl; add chicken and stir to coat. Cover and chill overnight.
3. When the chicken is marinated, heat olive oil in a large heavy pot over medium heat. Add the other half of the spices and let them 'toast'

for a few seconds, then add onion, tomato paste, cardamom, and cook, stirring often, until tomato paste has darkened and onion is soft, about 5 minutes.

4. Add marinated chicken (including marinade), and diced tomatoes. Bring to a simmer, stirring often, and cook for about 15 minutes. Add the coconut milk and simmer slowly for an extra 5 minutes.

5. Salt to taste. Sprinkle with cilantro and serve with brown basmati or jasmine rice, and vegetables.

TIMESAVER: Prepare ahead: Chicken can be made 2 days ahead. Cover and chill. Reheat before serving.

SERVING INFO: 590 calories, 29g fat, 19g carbohydrates, 62g protein, 4g fiber, 9g sugar

CHICKEN TERIYAKI

Active time: 30 minutes | **Cook time:** 1 hour | **Yield:** 4 servings

INGREDIENTS:

8 skinless chicken thighs

1 tsp cornstarch

1 tbsp cold water

2 tbsps hoisin sauce

1 tbsp Truvia®

½ cup (gluten-free) soy sauce

¼ cup cider vinegar

1 clove garlic, minced

1 tsp fresh ginger, grated

¼ tsp ground black pepper

In this cookbook I've tried to create recipes that fit your busy lifestyle. I love 2-step recipes that take no time to prep, burn fat, and have tons of flavor. This is definitely one of them.

This version has been modified for burning fat. Yet, it's extremely close to the traditional Japanese technique, which consists of broiling or grilling meat with a glaze made of soy sauce, mirin, and sugar. The Japanese word "tare" refers to the glaze, while "yaki" refers to the grilling technique. Here is the Japanese lesson of the day for you!

QUICK TIP: If you have time to marinate the chicken overnight before cooking, you will have a deeper, even more flavorful dish. In fact, if you add a little unsweetened pineapple juice (say ½ cup), its enzymes will help tenderize the chicken.

PREPARATION:

1. Preheat oven to 400° (200°c). In a small saucepan over low heat, combine the cornstarch, cold water, hoisin sauce, Truvia®, soy sauce, vinegar, garlic, ginger and ground black pepper. Let simmer, stirring frequently, until sauce thickens a bit and bubbles.
2. Place chicken pieces in an ovenproof dish. Pour sauce over. Bake in the preheated oven for 30 minutes. Serve hot.

SERVING INFO: 310 calories, 16g fat, 9g carbohydrates, 29g protein, 3g fiber, 4g sugar

CHICKEN MARSALA

Active time: 10 minutes | **Cook time:** 20 minutes | **Yield:** 4 servings

INGREDIENTS:

4 skinless, boneless chicken breasts, pounded ¼ inch thick

¼ cup coconut flour for coating

1 tsp dried oregano

3 tbsps extra-virgin olive oil

1 cup sliced mushrooms

½ cup diced onions

¼ cup Marsala wine

¼ cup low-sodium chicken stock

1 tbsp whipping cream

2 tbsps Italian parsley, chopped

1 tsp paprika

½ tsp cayenne pepper

salt and pepper to taste

Why are there so many versions of Chicken Marsala? Because it's delicious. Marsala is the name of a Sicilian wine. Chicken breast is coated with flour, sauteed with mushrooms, then the Marsala reduction is made. I like to pound the chicken to tenderize it, and so the sauce penetrates the meat, resulting in amazing texture and flavor. I stripped this recipe of its fat and empty calorie content. I did, however, keep a tiny bit of cream, which is important to bind the sauce into a delicious texture.

QUICK TIP: It's important to control the heat during the sautéing process. When you 'sauté' something, make sure the pan is hot and add just enough extra-virgin olive oil to barely coat the pan. Also make sure the chicken is dry, as moisture demotes the making of the nice crust we all love. You'll know you've added the chicken to the pan at the right time (presentation side down) when you hear the characteristic sizzling sound. Pssshhhhht!

PREPARATION:

1. In a shallow dish or bowl, mix together the flour, salt, pepper, paprika, cayenne, and oregano. Coat chicken pieces in flour mixture.
2. In a large skillet, heat oil over medium-high heat. Sear chicken in the hot pan, and lightly brown. Turn over chicken pieces, brown, and set aside. Add onions and mushrooms to the pan and sauté until brown. Pour in wine and stock. Bring chicken back to the pan and cover skillet. Simmer chicken 10 minutes, turning once, until no longer pink and juices run clear.
3. Transfer chicken to serving platter. Add cream to the sauce; boil to reduce it by half until it thickens a bit. Pour the sauce over chicken and serve hot.

SERVING INFO: 249 calories, 16 fat, 25g carbohydrates, 19g protein, 11g fiber, 13g sugar

ORANGE CHICKEN

Active time: 25 minutes | **Cook time:** 15 minutes | **Yield:** 4 servings

INGREDIENTS:

Sauce:

½ cup water

2 tbsps orange juice

2 tbsps lemon juice

1 tbsp rice vinegar

2 tbsps gluten-free soy sauce

1 tbsp grated orange zest

1 tbsp Truvia®

½ cup hoisin sauce

½ tsp minced fresh ginger root

½ tsp minced garlic

2 tbsps chopped green onion

¼ tsp red pepper flakes

Chicken:

2 boneless, skinless chicken breasts, cut into ½-inch strips

1 cup coconut flour

1 tsp cornstarch

2 tbsps sesame oil

salt and pepper to taste

If you go to your local mall, chances are you'll find a restaurant serving the popular orange chicken. Mine is a delicious recipe with flavors reminiscent of citrus. It's one of my favorite and a go-to dish for family dinner time.

Typically, this Chinese-American classic involves chopped, battered, and fried chicken pieces coated in a very sweet orange-flavored spicy glaze. I removed most of the sugar and avoided deep-frying. Instead, the natural orange and lemon flavors the meat. Ginger, garlic, and red pepper add another dimension and contribute to this extraordinary fat-burning dish. In other words, you have the best of both worlds—a truly delicious dish that will help you stay fit.

PREPARATION:

1. Pour the water, orange juice, lemon juice, rice vinegar, and soy sauce into a saucepan and set over medium-high heat. Stir in the orange zest, Truvia®, hoisin sauce, ginger, garlic, chopped onion, and red pepper flakes. Bring to a boil. Remove from heat, and cool 10 to 15 minutes.

2. In a resealable plastic bag, mix the flour, cornstarch, salt, and pepper, and the chicken pieces, seal the bag, and shake to coat.

3. Heat the olive oil in a large skillet over medium-high heat. Remove excess flour, and place chicken into the skillet to brown. When nice and brown, remove chicken and set aside. Add the sauce to the pan and simmer over medium-high heat. Reduce heat to medium low, add the chicken pieces back in the pan, and simmer for 5 minutes. Serve hot.

HEALTHY SOUTHERN FRIED CHICKEN

Active time: 35 minutes (plus marinating time) | **Cook time:** 25 minutes | **Yield:** 4 servings

INGREDIENTS:

4 boneless chicken thighs

4 chicken breasts, cut in half crosswise

1 quart buttermilk

4 cloves garlic, minced

3 sprigs rosemary, stem off and minced

3 sprigs thyme, steam off and minced

2 bay leaves

zest and juice from 1 lemon

2 cups coconut flour

½ tsp cayenne pepper

1 tsp paprika

2 cups unsweetened, whole-grain cereals (such as Ezekiel or Bob's Red Mill), processed into crumbs

4 egg whites, lightly beaten

salt and pepper to taste

If you've been watching your nutrition for a while, chances are you can't even remember the taste of fried chicken. Who can blame you? Deep-frying breaded foods, even if done well, are a nightmare in terms of proper nutrition.

Rejoice! I have tweaked this classic recipe into a healthy version and you'd never know it. The first step toward really good fried chicken is a great marinade. My buttermilk marinade tenderizes the chicken and brings an aromatic and tangy flavor to it.

I also replace breadcrumbs (often made of white bread) with a more nutritious option. Instead of empty calorie breading, you get a full serving of fiber and nutrients. Finally, I ditch the deep-frying. There's no need to saturate the breading with fat. Instead, the chicken is delicately coated, then roasted to a golden brown crust.

QUICK TIP: Using cooking spray to coat chicken pieces just before baking them will help give your fried chicken a nice golden color.

PREPARATION:

1. Combine the buttermilk, salt, garlic, rosemary, thyme, bay leaves, lemon zest and juice. Add the chicken to the buttermilk brine and cover; refrigerate for at least 4 hours or overnight.

2. Preheat oven to 350° (180°c). Mix flour, paprika, and cayenne pepper. Remove the chicken from the brine and pat dry. Dredge the chicken in the flour mixture, making sure that every piece is coated evenly with flour. Place egg whites in a resealable plastic bag and add the chicken to coat. Place 'breadcrumbs' in a resealable plastic bag and add the chicken to coat. Finally, transfer the chicken to a baking sheet. Arrange in one layer.

3. Roast chicken in the oven until brown and crispy, about 25 minutes. Temperature inside the thigh should read 165° (73°c). Serve hot.

12-HOUR TIMESAVER: The buttermilk marinade infuses a lot of flavor into this dish. In a hurry? You'll have an acceptable result if you skip the overnight marinating and go straight to step 2.

OPTIONS: If buttermilk is just not your thing, you can either replace with milk, or just skip the liquid and marinate the chicken in the spices with a tbsp of extra-virgin olive oil.

SERVING INFO: 450 calories, 25g fat, 4g carbohydrates, 48g protein, 1g fiber, 2g sugar

SALISBURY STEAK

Active time: 15 minutes | **Cook time:** 20 minutes | **Yield:** 4 servings

INGREDIENTS:

2 lbs. 90% lean ground beef

1 cup leftover French onion soup (page 58)

1 egg, lightly beaten

2 tbsps tomato paste

2 tsps Worcestershire sauce, to taste

1 tsp Dijon mustard

¼ cup water

salt and pepper to taste

You've seen it in the frozen section of your grocery store, and you've heard the name many times. Salisbury Steak. An American physician and early advocate of low-carb weight control diets invented it in 1888! Apparently, he recommended his patients eat Salisbury steaks three times a day! I'm not sure about that often, but once in a while, you should probably revisit this delicious high-protein classic dish.

QUICK TIP: Make sure you choose beef that is 90% protein and only 10% fat.

PREPARATION:

1. In a large bowl, mix together ⅓ cup leftover French onion soup with ground beef, egg, salt and black pepper. Shape into 4 oval patties.

2. In a large skillet over medium-high heat, brown both sides of patties. Pour off excess fat. Set the steaks aside on paper towels and pat dry to remove additional fat.

3. In a small bowl, blend remaining soup with tomato paste, water, Worcestershire sauce and Dijon mustard. Pour over meat in skillet. Cover, and simmer for 15 minutes, stirring occasionally. Serve hot.

BEEF AND BROCCOLI STIR-FRY

Active time: 15 minutes | **Cook time:** 10 minutes | **Yield:** 4 servings

INGREDIENTS:

1 pound boneless flank steak, cut into thin 3-inch strips

2 tsps cornstarch

1 tsp minced garlic

2 tsps sesame seeds

2 tbsps toasted sesame oil

4 cups broccoli florets

1 small onion, cut into wedges

⅓ cup (gluten-free) soy sauce

2 tsps Truvia®

1 tsp ginger, minced

juice of 1 lemon

hot cooked, long-grain rice

PREPARATION:

1. In a bowl, combine sesame seeds, beef, and cornstarch, then toss.
2. In a large skillet or wok over medium high heat, stir-fry beef in 1 tbsp oil until beef reaches desired doneness; remove and set aside. Do not overcrowd the pan and work in batches, if necessary.
3. Over high heat, stir-fry broccoli and onion in remaining oil for 4-5 minutes. Return beef to pan.
4. Add soy sauce, molasses, Truvia®, garlic, ginger and 1 tbsp of lemon juice until smooth. Cook and stir for 2 minutes. Serve hot

FAV

BEST. STEAK. EVER.

Active time: 20 minutes | **Cook time:** 10-14 minutes | **Yield:** 4 servings

INGREDIENTS:

4 8-oz beef tenderloin steaks, preferably prime and dry aged

6 tbsps paprika

2 tbsps cayenne pepper

5 tbsps freshly ground black pepper

6 tbsps garlic powder

3 tbsps onion powder

2 tbsps dried thyme

kosher salt to taste

1 tbsp extra-virgin olive oil

When I was teaching at culinary school, an awkward, young, and passionate student presented me with a dry rub recipe. I must admit I didn't have high hopes for it, but I didn't want to disappoint him, so I agreed to try it in class.

The next day we made the rub, put it on the steak, and grilled it. After we cut into the perfectly cooked meat and took the first bite we were blown away. It was the most amazing steak I ever tasted. When you prepare this recipe for your friends and family you'll hear over and over, "Best. Steak. Ever." Soon you'll be known as the King of the Grill.

QUICK TIP: After you grill the steak, let it rest for about half the cooking time. That will rehydrate the meat with its juices and will produce a moist and incredibly tender steak.

PREPARATION:

1. Make the rub. Mix together paprika, cayenne pepper, black pepper, garlic powder, onion powder, and dried thyme. Do not add salt.
2. Pat the steaks dry with a paper towel to remove any excess moisture, then season generously with the rub. Wrap the steak in plastic wrap and refrigerate for at least 4 hours but preferably overnight.
3. Bring the steaks to room temperature, about one hour. Fifteen minutes before grilling, salt the steak generously (undersalting is a common beginner mistake). Rub the steak with just enough olive oil to coat.
4. Place the steaks on a very hot grill. Control the heat and refrain from moving the meat. Do not cover or close the grill top. After about a minute of grilling, move the steaks 90 degrees on the same side to make the traditional "criss-cross" grillmarks. After another minute, you can flip the steak, grill for one minute, and then close the grill until desired doneness.
5. Transfer steak to a cutting board and allow to rest for half its cooking time. Garnish with a finishing salt such as fleur de sel, if desired. Serve immediately after resting time.

Steak Doneness	Remove From Grill at This Temperature	Final Cooked Temperature
RARE	125°	130°
MEDIUM RARE	135°	140°
MEDIUM	145°	150°
WELL DONE	I'M NOT TALKING TO YOU	GO AWAY

TIMESAVER: No time saver here. This is your shot to greatness and we are not taking shortcuts.

OPTIONS: Any steak is great steak, as you know, and any steak works well with this rub recipe. If you are on a budget, go for skirt, flank, or flat iron steak. If you want to break the bank to impress your friends and family, indulge in filet mignon or Craig Ballantyne's favorite, the rib eye steak.

SURPRISE BONUS: This rub also tastes amazing on chicken, pork, and even fish!

SERVING INFO: 630 calories, 14g fat, 79 carbohydrates, 23g fiber, 51g protein, 8g sugar

BLACK KALE CHILI

Active time: 10 minutes | **Cook time:** 30 minutes to 1 hour | **Yield:** 4 servings

INGREDIENTS:

1 onion, chopped

2 tsps chili powder

3 small cans kidney beans, drained

1 bunch of black kale, stems off

1 pound 90% ground beef

2 tbsps tomato paste

1 medium can of diced tomatoes

1 cup water

Can you think of an easier comfort food than chili con carne? I add black kale to mine because I love its fiber and vitamins, and because it looks good. My recipe here will give you an awesome tasting chili con carne. Make a huge batch. That way you'll have leftovers for the next few days, or you can portion and freeze for another time. Chili keeps well in the freezer. In a previous recipe I introduced the simple principle of chemistry called osmosis and diffusion. Things you start cooking in a cold environment and bring to a simmer, exchange flavors better than things you start in a hot environment and cook for the same amount of time. This means your chili will taste better the next day. Why? Because when you make the recipe once, the flavors are predictable. But if you cool the chili, and then bring it to a simmer, the above chemistry applies, and each ingredient efficiently exchanges flavors with the others. Your chili tastes better than it did the day you prepared it. For that reason, just like soups, stews, and casseroles, this chili is best the next day. Don't hesitate to serve it as a leftover.

QUICK TIP: The more you cook chili, the better it is. If you have time, simmer it slowly for two or three hours.

PREPARATION:

4. Over medium-high heat, cook the onions and the chili powder until onions are soft and translucent.
5. Add the beef and brown. Stir from time to time to break it up with your spatula. Add tomato paste, kidney beans, water, kale, and tomatoes.
6. Bring to a boil, give it a good stir and cover. Turn down the heat and simmer for at least 30 minutes, preferably 1 hour or more. Serve with brown rice.

OPTIONS: Add sweet peppers or spice it up with poblano peppers or jalapenos. Tomatillos are a good addition for a variation of chili verde (green chile).

For a vegetarian option, replace the beef with chopped vegetables (zucchini, celery, carrots, broccoli, etc.).

SERVING INFO: 570 calories, 25g fat, 52g protein, 33g carbohydrates, 5g fiber, 17g sugar

OLD-FASHIONED MEATLOAF

Active time: 15 minutes | **Cook time:** 1 hour | **Yield:** 4 servings

INGREDIENTS:

2 lbs. 90% lean ground beef

½ cup unsweetened, whole-grain cereals (Ezekiel or Bob's Red Mill brands), processed into crumbs

1 egg

1 onion, finely chopped

3 tbsps tomato paste

⅔ cup low-fat milk

Sauce:

4 tbsps apple cider vinegar

2 tbsps molasses

2 tsps Worcestershire sauce

½ cup tomato paste

salt and pepper to taste

This is another ultra-fast, fat-burning recipe you'll just love because it will save you time in the kitchen. When I see recipes listing dozens of ingredients and an ultra-long preparation list I feel like giving up and doing something else instead. With this recipe, however, your meatloaf will be roasting in the oven in no time so you can focus on something else, like preparing another recipe or going out to play. Either way, you'll love this.

QUICK TIP: In meatloaf recipes, breadcrumbs serve the purpose of softening the texture of the loaf. More meat means more flavor, but the meatloaf will feel drier and chewier. The ratio of meat to breadcrumbs is important.

PREPARATION:
1. Combine all meat loaf ingredients, place into an ovenproof dish, and shape into a log.
2. Combine sauce ingredients and pour on top and sides of meatloaf.
3. Bake at 350° (180°c) about 45 minutes to 1 hour.

OPTIONS: You can skip the 'breadcrumbs,' or replace them with gluten-free breadcrumbs.

SUPERMEATBALLS

Active time: 20 minutes | **Cook time:** 45 minutes | **Yield:** 4 servings

INGREDIENTS:

For the supermeatballs:

1 lb. of ground bison meat

1 lb. of 90% lean ground beef

1 lb. of ground veal or ground pork

1 cup unsweetened, whole-grain cereals (such as Ezekiel or Bob's Red Mill brand), processed into crumbs

6 thin slices of pancetta (Italian bacon)

6 cloves of garlic, minced

1 cup of part skim ricotta cheese

½ cup of Parmigiano-Reggiano, grated

½ cup of fresh herbs, finely chopped (use a blend of fresh Italian parsley, basil, oregano and sage)

1 tsp of cayenne pepper

1 tsp of paprika

1 tbsp extra-virgin olive oil

salt and pepper to taste

For the sauce:

2 medium cans of San Marzano diced tomatoes

1 cup red wine

6 ounces of part-skim mozzarella, sliced

1 onion, diced

6 cloves of garlic, minced

1 sprig of fresh oregano

salt and pepper to taste

These are not just meatballs. They're supermeatballs, another kind entirely, full of complex flavors and excellent texture. Preparing them may be a little more involved than most of my other recipes but trust me, it'll be worth the time.

PREPARATION:

1. Lay the pancetta on a baking sheet and bake in a preheated oven 375° (177°c), until brown and crispy, about 25 minutes. Let cool and chop with a chef knife.
2. Mix all supermeatball ingredients together (including pancetta but excluding olive oil) and knead until well blended.
3. Wet your hands and shape large 4-ounce balls. Meanwhile, heat up a roasting pan over medium-high heat and lightly coat with extra-virgin olive oil.

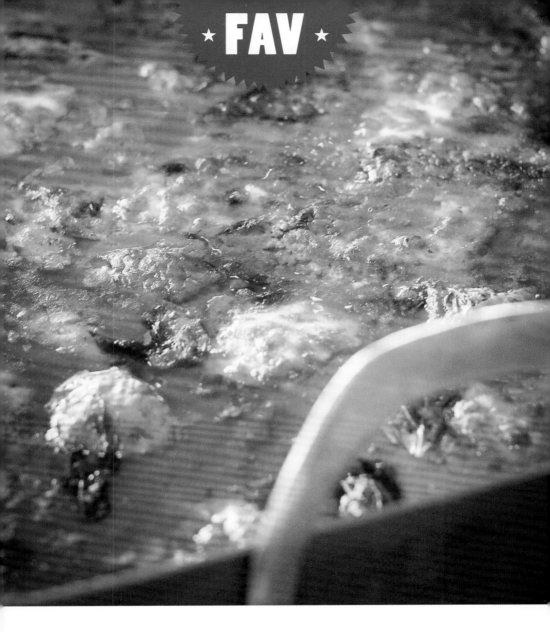

4. When all meatballs are shaped, start searing them in the roasting pan. You want to make a nice crust so don't overcrowd the pan and work in batches, if necessary.

5. When all meatballs are seared, add the sauce ingredients, topping with the mozzarella.

6. Bake in the oven for at least 30 minutes, preferably 45 minutes to 1 hour.

15-MINUTE TIMESAVER: Skipping step 4 will save you about 15 minutes.

SERVING INFO: 340 calories, 23g fat, 12g carbohydrates, 21g ... fiber 7g ...

CUBAN PICADILLO

Active time: 20 minutes | **Cook time:** 30 minutes | **Yield:** 4 servings

INGREDIENTS:

2 lbs. 90% lean ground beef

1 hot Italian sausage or chorizo, casing removed

1 tbsp extra-virgin olive oil

2 onions, chopped

4 cloves garlic, minced

1 medium can diced tomatoes

2 tbsps red-wine vinegar

1 tbsp ground cinnamon

2 tsps ground cumin

2 bay leaves

pinch of ground cloves

pinch of nutmeg

⅔ cup raisins

⅔ cup pitted stuffed olives

salt and pepper to taste

Picadillo is a great dish originally from Cuba, but present in the Caribbean and all over Latin America, too. It's an aromatic stew of ground beef and tomatoes. Raisins add sweetness and olives add a little saltiness. Its flavor is reminiscent of sofrito, chorizo, cinnamon and cumin, as well as other spices.

I really encourage you to try this recipe. It's one of my best and it's addictive.

PREPARATION:

1. Heat up a large skillet over medium-high heat. When hot, add onions, chorizo and garlic, and cook until the onions are soft and translucent, about10 minutes.

2. Add beef and brown, crumbling the meat with a spatula. Salt and pepper to taste.

3. Add tomatoes, vinegar, cinnamon, cumin, bay leaves, cloves and nutmeg and stir to combine. Simmer, covered, for approximately 25 minutes.

4. Uncover the pan, and add the raisins and olives. Cook for another 15 minutes. Serve with cooked brown rice or another side.

COUNTRY-STYLE BBQ RIBS

Active time: 25 minutes | **Cook time:** 2 hours | **Yield:** 4 servings

INGREDIENTS:

3 lbs. country style pork ribs

1 cup tomato paste

1 cup water

½ cup apple cider vinegar

1 tbsp molasses

2 tsps onion powder

1 tbsp Dijon mustard

1 tbsp Worcestershire sauce

1 tsp liquid smoke

You may think that BBQ ribs are out of the picture for you, but they don't have to be, especially if you give my recipe a try. How are they different from the 'fatty' style found in most restaurants? First, I use country-style pork ribs, which come from one of the leanest areas of the pig. That makes a big difference! Second, instead of roasting, I rub and simmer my ribs until tender, then slowly roast with a sauce that has been stripped of all unhealthy items--yet still packed with flavor!

QUICK TIP: Everybody needs a little tenderness! Make sure the ribs gently simmer in the broth, instead of boiling hard. That's important to keep all the collagen in the meat, which results in very tender ribs.

PREPARATION:

1. Place ribs in a large pot and cover with water. Bring water to a gentle simmer, and cook ribs until tender, about one hour.
2. For the sauce, mix all other ingredients in a saucepan and boil for 5 minutes.
3. Preheat oven to 325° (165°c). Remove ribs from pot, drain the water, pat dry, and place them in a baking dish. Pour barbeque sauce over ribs. Cover with aluminum foil and bake in the preheated oven for 1 hour.

TIMESAVER: No time saver tip here. BBQ ribs need to cook slow, slow, slow...

SERVING INFO: 270 calories, 9g fat, 17g carbohydrates, 27g protein, 2g fiber, 12g sugar

PORK TENDERLOIN ROAST WITH CARAMELIZED APPLES

Active time: 20 minutes | **Cook time:** 30 minutes | **Yield:** 4 servings

INGREDIENTS:

2 pork tenderloins

2 lbs. apples, peeled, cored, and quartered

3 tbsps extra-virgin olive oil

½ tsp dried thyme

½ tsp dried oregano

1 tbsp fresh ginger, grated

3 tbsps coconut flour

1 cup dry white wine

salt and pepper to taste

Pork tenderloin is a very interesting meat to cook. It can turn out moist, soft, and very tender, or it can easily become overcooked and dry. Read on for some of the best cooking tips you'll ever receive. The blessing and the curse is that pork tenderloin is a very lean meat, making it a great fat-burning item to add to your cooking repertoire. A lean meat is more difficult to cook, though. It requires stopping the cooking process at the right time to prevent overcooking, and that's a little tricky. Pork also gets a bad rep because of old tales recommending one cook it to death—or else!

I recommend cooking pork tenderloin to a medium rare, and let 'carryover cooking' (the cooking still occurring in a larger piece of meat once it's taken away from the heat source) work its magic. At that point the pork tenderloin gently keeps on cooking to a nice medium temperature, and its natural juices rehydrate every muscle fiber. The result is a melt-in-your-mouth piece of meat that has little to do with the pork tenderloin you've probably had all your life. Give this a try.

QUICK TIP: Monitor the pork tenderloin instead of relying on cooking time. The best way to see if it's cooked is to press it with your (clean) fingers. It should feel soft, tender, and a bit bouncy. Your fingers should spring back a bit.

PREPARATION:

1. Preheat oven to 350° (180°c). Rub the tenderloins with dried herbs.
2. In a heavy skillet over medium high heat, sear the pork to brown with the olive oil, about 3 minutes on each side.
3. Add ginger and apples, and brown over medium-high heat. Do not move the apples too much; we want them to brown.
4. Add coconut flour and stir to coat the apples and the pork. Immediately add 1 cup of wine and bake at 350° (180°c) for about 15 minutes. Take pork out of the oven, rest 10 minutes, and slice to serve.

SERVING INFO: 600 calories, 42g fat, 53g protein, 9g carbohydrates, 2g fiber, 8g sugar

BRAISED PORK WITH WHITE WINE AND CARROTS

Active time: 20 minutes | **Cook time:** 45 minutes | **Yield:** 4 servings

INGREDIENTS:

6 boneless pork shoulders, cubed

16 Kalamata olives

2 carrots, unpeeled and sliced

2 sprigs thyme

1 bay leaf

1 sprig of Italian parsley leaves, chopped

6 garlic cloves, peeled

2 tbsps extra-virgin olive oil

4 tbsps coconut flour

2 cups white wine

2 cups low-sodium chicken broth

salt and pepper to taste

Braising is my absolute favorite cooking method. It combines the delicious flavor of searing (the action of making a nice crust on the meat) and simmering in a broth, which makes tough meat tender. Pork shoulder acquires a melt-in-your-mouth softness that you will absolutely love.

QUICK TIP: Everybody needs a little tenderness! Make sure the meat gently simmers in the broth, instead of boiling hard. That's important to keep all the collagen in the meat, which results in very tender meat.

PREPARATION:

1. Season pork with salt and pepper. Heat up a skillet over medium-high heat. When hot, add just enough oil to coat the bottom of the pan, about 1 tbsp. Sear the pork until brown, working in batches. It's important to refrain from moving the meat around; you want it to brown. Add the garlic cloves to the pan and sauté until golden brown, 1 to 2 minutes.

2. Sprinkle the mixture with the flour and stir over low heat until golden brown, about 1 minute. Add the wine and bring it to a simmer, scraping the pan with a wooden spoon to pull up the brown bits, until reduced by one-third. Add the stock, browned garlic cloves, carrots, olives and herbs to the pan. Simmer covered for 30 minutes.

3. Serve hot and sprinkle with chopped parsley.

20-MINUTE TIMESAVER: While browning the meat is important, skipping that step will save you about 20 minutes.

SERVING INFO: 330 calories, 5g fat, 20g carbohydrates, 49g protein, 2g fiber, 14g sugar

SWEET AND SPICY ROAST PORK

Active time: 20 minutes | **Cook time:** 30 minutes | **Yield:** 4 servings

INGREDIENTS:

2 lbs. of pork tenderloin, in large cubes

1 lemon, freshly squeezed

3 tbsps orange juice

1 tbsp whole-grain mustard

2 tbsps honey

1 bay leaf

1 tsp crushed red pepper flakes

3 cups carrots, washed, unpeeled, and sliced

1 onion, halved and thinly sliced

2 scallions, thinly sliced, for garnish

salt and pepper to taste

It's spicy but not overly so. It's sweet but subtle. It's tangy like citrus. This is your brand new Sweet and Spicy Roast Pork recipe. Pork tenderloin is one of the leanest meats around so feel free to indulge in this fat-burning powerhouse. I recommend not peeling the carrots in order to add much needed fiber to your diet. Ingredients can easily be assembled up to 24 hours in advance. If you have guests, all you need to do is place the roast in the oven when the guests arrive and garnish it at the last minute.

PREPARATION:

1. In a saucepan, whisk together lemon juice, orange juice, mustard, honey, salt, bay leaf, red pepper flakes and black pepper to taste. Bring to a boil and simmer for 5 minutes. Let cool.
2. Put pork in a bowl and add honey mixture. Add carrots, onion, and thyme. Marinate at least 30 minutes at room temperature, but preferably overnight in the refrigerator.
3. Heat oven to 425° (218°c). Transfer all ingredients, including marinade, to an ovenproof dish. Roast until pork is slightly browned and cooked through, about 15-20 minutes.
4. Serve hot and sprinkle with scallions.

OPTIONS:

1. This dish can be made with chicken, as well.
2. For natural sweetness add dried fruits such as dates, apricots, or plums.

SERVING INFO: 330 calories, 18g fat, 22g carbohydrates, 20g protein, 7g fiber, 12g sugar

PORK THAI CURRY

Active time: 10 minutes | **Cook time:** 20 minutes | **Yield:** 4 servings

INGREDIENTS:

For the curry paste:

3 shallots, minced

4 garlic cloves, minced

2 tbsps fresh ginger, minced

1 tbsp extra-virgin olive oil

2 tsps curry powder

1 tsp turmeric

1 tsp ground cumin

cayenne pepper 1 tsp

salt to taste

For the pork:

1 lb. pork tenderloin, cubed

1 cup low-sodium chicken stock

1 small can coconut milk

1 lb. rutabaga, cut into ⅓-inch pieces

1 onion, diced

⅓ cup peanuts, toasted

¼ cup chopped fresh cilantro

salt and pepper to taste

This pork dish is sweet and savory and at the same time, a bit spicy. It is reminiscent of the traditional Thai curries, with shallots, ginger, and garlic. This recipe is for a mild yellow curry. Did you know that most Thai curries are identified by their colors? Red curries are moderately salty-sweet, spicy and sour with a drizzle of lime juice. Green curries contain green chilies, raw aromatics like ginger, and are generally very hot. Yellow curries, on the other hand, are mostly mild and are heavy on turmeric, which creates the yellow color.

Many curry recipes call for a very long list of spices. I like simplicity, so I cut down on the spices for your convenience, keeping the identity of this awesome dish. The rutabaga is a smart addition! It looks and tastes like a potato, and adds a little sweetness.

QUICK TIP: Toast the spices (heat them up in the pan) to concentrate their inherent flavors for a full release of their pungency. It makes all the difference.

PREPARATION:

1. Heat oil in large saucepan over medium heat. Add all curry paste ingredients and cook, stirring constantly, until paste begins to brown, 2 to 3 minutes. Add pork and brown on all sides.
2. Stir in broth, rutabaga, onion, and peanuts, scraping up any browned bits. Bring to simmer and cook until vegetables are barely tender, about 15 minutes.
3. Sprinkle with cilantro and serve with basmati or jasmine brown rice.

SERVING INFO: 320 calories, 14g fat, 2g carbohydrates, 42g protein, 0g fiber, 2g sugar

SIMPLE MAHI WITH SESAME SOY SAUCE

Active time: 15 minutes | **Cook time:** 15 minutes | **Yield:** 4 servings

INGREDIENTS:

2 lbs. Mahi-Mahi

3 tbsps toasted sesame oil

3 tbsps rice vinegar

2 tbsps (gluten-free) soy sauce

2 tsps chili oil

1 sprig of cilantro, chopped

1 tsp of garlic, minced

1 tsp of fresh ginger, minced

This simple dish relies on quality ingredients. So buy quality ingredients, when possible. And use your creativity. Whisk in a little chili oil or a pinch of chili flakes, or a tsp of grated ginger or garlic.

QUICK TIP: Many of the soy sauces available in supermarkets are of low quality. If you have time, and if you so desire, go to an Asian store and buy the best soy sauce your money can buy. It makes a big difference.

PREPARATION:

1. Whisk together the sesame oil, rice vinegar, soy sauce, chili oil, garlic, ginger, and cilantro. Set aside.
2. Preheat broiler.
3. Pour a little sauce over the fish.
4. Place the fish on an ovenproof dish, and put under broiler. Cook the fish for a few minutes on each side, until it becomes opaque. Don't let the fish overcook. The entire process will only take a few minutes.
5. To serve, pour the rest of the sauce over the fish, and serve immediately.

OPTIONS: Any white fish can be prepared in the same way. Mahi-Mahi is great, but try grouper, sea bass, cod, or even tilapia. This broiling technique is so easy that it might become your go-to cooking method for fish.

GRILLED MARINATED SHRIMP

Active time: 25 minutes | **Cook time:** 5 minutes | **Yield:** 4 servings

INGREDIENTS:

2 lbs. large shrimp, peeled and deveined with tails on

¼ cup extra-virgin olive oil

¼ cup Italian parsley, chopped

1 lemon, juiced

2 tbsps hot sauce

3 cloves garlic, minced

1 tbsp tomato paste

2 tsps dried oregano

salt and pepper to taste

wooden skewers, soaked in water

limes or lemons, quartered, for presentation

Are you a deveiner or not? As a general rule, I always devein shrimp for my clients. At home I like to leave the shrimp intact, unpeeled and un-deveined. If the head is on, then it's even better. Why? Simply because the shell adds a ton of flavor. It keeps the moisture in, as the meat gently cooks, and amplifies the taste! I may not convince you and that's okay. The bottom line is that any shrimp is a good shrimp, especially if it's big and meaty. Go with jumbo!

QUICK TIP: Shrimp tell you when they're cooked; they change color. And that's all there is to it. Do not overcook them.

PREPARATION:

1. In a mixing bowl, mix together olive oil, parsley, lemon juice, hot sauce, garlic, tomato paste, oregano, salt, and pepper. Pour marinade into a large resealable plastic bag with shrimp. Seal, chill, and marinate for 2 hours.
2. Preheat grill on medium-low. Skewer shrimp, piercing once near the tail and once near the head. Discard marinade.
3. Lightly oil the grill grate. Cook shrimp for 5 minutes per side, or until they change color. Serve at once.

2-HOUR TIMESAVER: If you're running out of time, it's ok to skip the 2-hour marination. You can use an instant marinade.

COCONUT SHRIMP

Active time: 10 minutes | **Cook time:** 10 minutes | **Yield:** 4 servings

INGREDIENTS:

24 jumbo shrimp

2 egg whites

½ cup coconut flour

1 cup club soda

2 tsps baking powder

2 cups unsweetened, flaked coconut

1 tbsp of coconut oil

Did you know that when you deep-fry a breaded item, about 10% of the deep-frying oil stays with the item you eat? That's a lot of fat. And that's one of the reasons why I eliminated deep-frying from my diet. Instead, I prefer baking or broiling, which can give a result close to what you'd expect from a deep-fried item. The actual deep-frying technique is only part of the problem, though. Take coconut shrimp for instance. Processed versions (usually in the frozen section of your supermarket) are high-carb food items loaded with empty calories and ingredients you can't even pronounce. Imitating the process is not that difficult. I make a healthy batter with coconut flour, cover the shrimp with unsweetened coconut flakes, and bake the shrimp at high temperature to give them a little color.

Important: make sure you don't use sweetened coconut flakes. These are usually meant as a baking ingredient for cakes, and contain way too much sugar. Unsweetened coconut flakes are available in health food stores.

QUICK TIP: Try a simple horseradish dip (Greek yogurt and horseradish) to accompany these shrimp.

PREPARATION:

1. In medium bowl, combine egg white, coconut flour, club soda, and baking powder. Place coconut in a separate bowl.
2. Hold shrimp by tail, and dredge in batter, shaking off excess. Then roll shrimp in coconut, and place on a baking sheet lined with oiled parchment paper, in one layer. Refrigerate for 30 minutes. Meanwhile, preheat oven to 425° (218°c).
3. Bake shrimp in the oven, turning once with tongs, until golden brown. Serve warm.

GRILLED SALMON AND MANGO SALSA

Active time: 10 minutes | **Cook time:** 8 minutes | **Yield:** 4 servings

INGREDIENTS:

4 (8-ounce)
salmon fillets

2 mangoes, peeled
and diced

2 tbsps chopped
red onion

2 tbsps chopped fresh
tarragon

1 tsp red pepper flakes

salt and pepper
to taste

A grilled salmon can be phenomenal when cooked right. First of all, make sure the salmon is ultra fresh. The goal is to grill it just enough to cook it (salmon turns opaque and light pink) without overcooking it. We want it moist, tender, and flavorful. I recommend cooking 5 pieces instead of 4, and use one for testing its 'doneness.' When cut in its thickest part, the perfectly grilled salmon appears light pink throughout, with a center that is still moist and dark.

PREPARATION:

1. Combine mango, onions, tarragon, and crushed red pepper flakes. Cover and chill 1 hour.
2. On a hot grill, place fish and grill 4 minutes on each side, or until fish flakes easily when tested with a fork. Serve with mango salsa.

OPTIONS: Trout, arctic char, Coho salmon can all be prepared the same way. Other fish work very well when grilled: sea bass, grouper, halibut, tuna or swordfish. Serve with Caramelized Brussels Sprouts on page. 201.

SHRIMP AND GRITS

Active time: 15 minutes | **Cook time:** 20 minutes | **Yield:** 4 servings

INGREDIENTS:

2 lbs. large shrimp, peeled and deveined, tails intact

½ cup organic whole-grain steel cut grits

½ cup cauliflower florets, processed in food processor into "grits"

2 tbsps grated Parmigiano-Reggiano

1 tbsp extra-virgin olive oil

2 large cloves garlic, minced

1 large bunch kale, stem off

pinch of cayenne pepper

juice of 1 lemon, plus wedges for serving

2 tbsps Italian parsley, chopped

salt and pepper to taste

One would think that a high-carb item like Shrimp and Grits would be out of reach for anyone on a weight control or body-building plan. Depending on the actual ingredients and cooking techniques, however, it's not impossible to tip the scale the other way.

More often than not, burning fat is not just about the ingredients. It's about the quality of ingredients as well as the amount. If your shrimp and grits is all about instant grits (an empty calorie item) and a couple of shrimp, no need to even try the recipe. But let's say we actually cook more shrimp than grits. Then the protein intake in comparison to the carbohydrate intake becomes more favorable. Now add kale for fiber and vitamins, use a small amount of whole-grain, steel-cut grits (much higher in fiber and full of nutrients), and make 'fake grits' with cauliflower. Then the result is a completely acceptable dish for people watching their weight. And it goes without saying that the pleasure of such a delicious preparation is definitely a plus.

QUICK TIP: Cauliflower is a versatile vegetable. If you put florets in a food processor, and pulse it a few times, you will obtain tiny bits of cauliflower that look like real grits.

PREPARATION:

1. Bring 2 cups of water to a boil in a medium saucepan over high heat, covered. Uncover and slowly whisk in the grits, and salt and pepper. Reduce the heat to medium low and cook, stirring often, until thickened, about 20 minutes. You will need to add water as you go to keep the right consistency. When grits are cooked, stir in the kale until it wilts, then the cauliflower 'grits,' then the cheese. Remove from the heat and season with salt and pepper. Cover to keep warm.

2. Meanwhile, season the shrimp with salt and pepper. Heat up olive oil in a large skillet over medium-high heat. Add the shrimp, garlic and cayenne, and cook, tossing, until the shrimp change color, 3 to 4 minutes. Remove from the heat and add the lemon juice and parsley. Stir to coat the shrimp with the sauce and season with salt and pepper.

3. Divide the grits among shallow bowls and top with the shrimp and sauce. Serve with lemon wedges.

OPTIONS: Change the ratio of grits to 'cauliflower grits' according to your taste. You also can skip the grits for a most healthful meal.

SERVING INFO: 220 calories, 8g fat, 26g carbohydrates, 38g protein, 5g fiber, 3g sugar

SALMON BAKED IN FOIL

Active time: 15 minutes | **Cook time:** 25 minutes | **Yield:** 4 servings

INGREDIENTS:

4 salmon filets
(8 oz each)

2 beefsteak tomatoes,
chopped

1 onion, chopped

2 tbsps extra-virgin
olive oil

2 tbsps fresh
lemon juice

2 tsps fresh oregano

2 tsps fresh thyme

salt and pepper
to taste

As a sous chef, I would often arrive in the morning and make what the French call 'papillote,' [pap-uh-loht; French pa-pee-yawt] which may be the cutest word you'll ever say. I precut hundreds of aluminum sheets, making sure they were all the right size to allow for folding over the salmon. Then moving like an assembly line worker I'd add a piece of salmon and the tomato salsa, folding as I went. This recipe is fast and ideal for making ahead of time. Enjoy!

QUICK TIP: It is very important to fold the aluminum sheet properly. The seal must be tight. No air should leak as the foil pouch cooks and puffs up like a balloon. Then you can be sure the salmon is nicely steaming inside and the flavors mixing well.

PREPARATION:

1. Preheat the oven to 400° (200°c). Sprinkle salmon with salt and pepper. Stir the tomatoes, onions, oil, lemon juice, oregano, thyme, salt and pepper in a medium bowl to blend.

2. Place a salmon fillet atop a large sheet of foil (at least 8 x 11). Spoon ¼ of the tomato mixture over the salmon. Fold the sides of the foil over the fish and tomato mixture, covering completely; seal the packets closed. Place the foil packet on a heavy large baking sheet. Repeat until all of the salmon have been individually wrapped in foil and placed on the baking sheet.

3. Bake for 25 minutes. Using a large metal spatula, transfer the foil packets to plates and serve.

10-MINUTE TIMESAVER: This recipe can be made ahead. Prepare the packets in the morning, keep them in the refrigerator, and place in a preheated oven 25 minutes before dinner.

OPTIONS: Salmon is great for this recipe. But you can choose grouper, sea bass, cod, tilapia, and other fish, as well. Shrimp, scallops, clams or mussels, or any combination of fish and shellfish is just wonderful too. The cooking time remains the same as long as the pieces are not too big.

ULTRA-FAST TILAPIA BAKE

Active time: 5 minutes | **Cook time:** 30 minutes | **Yield:** 4 servings

INGREDIENTS:

4 tilapia filets
(6 oz each)

2 tsps extra-virgin
olive oil

1 tsp Old Bay
Seasoning

½ tsp garlic salt

1 lemon, sliced

2 cups cauliflower
florets

2 cups broccoli florets

1 red pepper, seeded
and diced

This easy and ultra-fast recipe will allow you to cook tilapia in a matter of minutes. It requires only a few ingredients.

QUICK TIP: You can also cook salmon, sea bass, cod, grouper, or other fish using the same method.

PREPARATION:

1. Preheat the oven to 375° (190°c). Oil an oven-proof baking dish, place the tilapia at the bottom, and drizzle with olive oil. Season with the spices. Top each one with a slice or two of lemon. Arrange the mixed vegetables around the fish, and season lightly with salt and pepper.

2. Cover the dish and bake for 25 minutes in the preheated oven, until vegetables are tender and fish flakes easily.

TIMESAVER: No time to go to the store? Make this recipe with a frozen piece of fish. Just increase the time by twenty-five percent.

BRITISH FISH AND CHIPS

Active time: 10 minutes | **Cook time:** 10 minutes | **Yield:** 4 servings

INGREDIENTS:

1½ lbs. Pacific cod fillet, cut into 4 pieces

1 cup coconut flour

2 tbsps baking powder

1 egg

2 egg whites, lightly beaten

½ cup Parmesan cheese

½ cup unsweetened whole-grain cereals (Ezekiel or Bob's Red Mill brand), processed into crumbs

½ tsp cayenne pepper

1 tsp paprika

2 tbsps olive oil

salt and pepper to taste

During my years in Oxford, England, as a young chef, I would get out after my shifts and bike around the active and gorgeous town of Oxford, stopping in pubs for a pint of bitter and an order of fish and chips. The dish includes salt and vinegar to season the chips (fries), and was served in an old newspaper! That was way back when.

I created this recipe for those who are craving a good fish and chips, yet can't indulge in the deep-fried version. Rutabaga fries (page 187) replace the chips, and a smart breading replaces the oily batter of the traditional dish.

PREPARATION:

1. Heat oven to 400° (200°c). Gather 3 medium bowls. In the first one, put the coconut flour, baking powder, paprika and cayenne. In the second one, put the eggs. In the third one, mix the Parmigiano-Reggiano and the cereal crumbs.

2. Also set up an oiled baking sheet. Working from left to right, dredge the pieces of fish in flour, shake to remove excess, then move to the egg whites, and cover the fish. Move the fish to the third bowl and cover with crumbs. Dip the fish one last time in the egg mixture. Finally, set on the baking sheet.

3. Bake the fish until the crust is nice, crisp, and golden, and the inside is just cooked through and opaque, about 10 minutes.

4. Serve with the faux fries on page 187.

MEXICAN CHILE RELLENOS

Active time: 30 minutes | **Cook time:** 20 minutes | **Yield:** 4 servings

INGREDIENTS:

8 fresh poblano chile peppers, halved lengthwise and seeded

1 lb. 90% lean ground beef

1 package Mexican cheese queso fresco, crumbled

1 onion, diced

4 garlic cloves, minced

½ cup cilantro, chopped

1 tsp chili powder

1 medium can of diced tomatoes

1 small can of black beans

1 cup of white wine

2 bay leaves

2 jalapeno peppers, sliced crosswise

salt and pepper to taste

This recipe is absolutely delicious. You'll want to double it because it's so good. It's my wife Carissa's favorite dish in this entire cookbook. Another reason for doubling it is because the following recipe (Chile Bolognese on page 159) uses the leftovers (if there are any). And the Chile Bolognese is something you won't want to miss. Before you start cooking, let me tell you about poblano chilies. They look like elongated sweet green peppers, but are a little darker in color. They're a bit spicy, but in a mild and subtle way.

PREPARATION:

1. Mix together beef, half of the queso fresco, onion, garlic, cilantro, chili powder, salt and pepper.
2. Stuff peppers with the beef and cheese mix, and place them on an oiled baking sheet.
3. Pour the tomatoes, black beans, and wine over and sprinkle with jalapeno slices. Top with remaining queso fresco. Bake at 350° (180°c) for about 45 minutes.
4. Serve hot.

OPTIONS: Of course, if even a mild poblano pepper scares you, you are welcome to use sweet peppers, green or red.

CHILE BOLOGNESE

Active time: 10 minutes | **Cook time:** 20 minutes | **Yield:** 8 servings

INGREDIENTS:

1½ lbs. (organic) whole-grain pasta fettuccine

3 ounces Parmigiano-Reggiano cheese, grated

Leftover chile rellenos (page 157)

1 small or medium can of diced tomatoes

How about a nice, rich, spicy twist on the classic Bolognese? The Mexican chile rellenos of page 157 are chopped up, mixed with the tomato sauce, and added to whole-grain pasta. I once worked in a kitchen with Gennaro, an Italian chef who made phenomenal potato gnocchi from scratch. I admired his skills and passion about food. I remember him showing me how to cook real al dente pasta, the way they cook it in Italy. You would not believe how firm the pasta was. If it wasn't coming from him, I would have said the pasta was undercooked. I later took a trip to Tuscany and I received confirmation of the real al dente.

QUICK TIP: The amount of time you cook pasta has an impact on fat loss. It turns out that al dente pasta has a much lower glycemic index than fully cooked pasta. Overcooking boosts the glycemic index. I recommend cooking pasta al dente, and even a couple of minutes less than what the manufacturer's package says. Cooked pasta should be slightly firm and offer some resistance when you chew it.

PREPARATION:

1. Pull the leftover stuffed peppers from the sauce and roughly chop them. Bring them back to the sauce.

2. In a large Dutch oven, reheat the chopped leftover peppers, sauce, a can of diced tomatoes and cook for 20 minutes. If you need more sauce, add another can of diced tomatoes. After it has cooked, process with a hand blender to smooth the sauce out.

3. While the sauce is cooking, bring a large pot of salted water to a boil. Add the pasta and cook until al dente. Drain the pasta. Do not rinse. Add the pasta to the sauce, and toss until it is well coated, about 3 minutes. Sprinkle Parmigiano-Reggiano over the pasta and serve.

TIMESAVER: Make ahead: Cool and refrigerate the sauce for up to four days.

CLASSIC PASTA A LA NORMA

Active time: 20 minutes | **Cook time:** 20 minutes | **Yield:** 4 servings

INGREDIENTS:

1 lb. whole-grain pasta

3 tbsps extra-virgin olive oil

4 cloves garlic, minced

2 eggplants, diced with skin on

1 medium can diced San Marzano tomatoes

2 cups packed basil leaves, torn

½ tsp crushed red pepper flakes

4 ounces Parmigiano-Reggiano, grated

salt and pepper to taste

Everyday Italian comfort food is simple, easy, and tasty. I re-engineered this classic for fat loss. Sure, this is a carb dish! However, by using the best natural ingredients out there, adding fiber, selecting whole-grain pasta, and smart cooking techniques, we are able to take Pasta a la Norma into the green.

Make sure you cook your pasta al dente (very firm) to help your fat loss efforts, and don't skip on the quality of ingredients. This classic from Sicily is one of the easiest and most satisfying to enjoy. Toasted garlic, sautéed eggplant, natural tomatoes, fresh basil and a dusting of Parmigiano-Reggiano is all it needs.

QUICK TIP: Look for cans of heirloom tomatoes from San Marzano, Italy in your grocery store. Heirlooms resemble elongated Romas and have an intense sweetness combined with a subtle acidity, which makes them the perfect tomatoes to work with.

PREPARATION:

1. In a large skillet, heat up the oil and quickly sauté the garlic until lightly browned. Immediately add the eggplant and cook, stirring occasionally until tender, about 10 minutes. The eggplant will soak up oil so add some as you go. Add tomatoes, salt and pepper, and simmer the sauce for 10 minutes.
2. Meanwhile, bring a large pot of salted water to a boil. Add pasta and cook until just al dente. Drain pasta. Do not rinse. Transfer to the tomato sauce and toss with the basil and red pepper flakes.
3. Transfer to a platter and serve with Parmigiano-Reggiano.

THE NEW ALFREDO SAUCE

Active time: 10 minutes | **Cook time:** 15 minutes | **Yield:** 4 servings

INGREDIENTS:

1 lb. whole-grain pasta

1 tbsp extra-virgin olive oil

2 cloves garlic, minced

2 tsps coconut flour

1 cup low-fat milk

½ cup grated Parmesan cheese, plus more for topping

3 tbsps chopped fresh basil

salt and pepper to taste

There are thousands of Alfredo sauce recipes out there. Very few are fat-burning, though. In my recipe, I replace traditional flour with coconut flour, providing a lot of fiber. I use low-fat milk instead of cream, only a tiny bit of Parmesan cheese, and I select whole- grain organic pasta, which I cook al dente to slow down digestion thereby improving fat loss. And here you thought Pasta Alfredo was out of reach!

QUICK TIP: As I said in a previous recipe, cooking pasta al dente has a much lower glycemic index (which has some impact on fat loss) than fully cooked pasta. In Italy, they eat pasta to a level of firmness you wouldn't even dare tasting. So go for it and don't be afraid to undercook your pasta.

PREPARATION:

1.   Heat the oil over medium heat. Add the garlic and cook until it is slightly browned, about 1 minute. Quickly add in the flour and stir with a wooden spoon to make a roux. Whisk in the milk, salt and pepper, whisking constantly until just thickened, about 4 minutes. Add the Parmigiano-Reggiano cheese; whisk until melted, about 1 minute. Stir in the chopped basil.

2.   Meanwhile, bring a large pot of salted water to a boil. Add the pasta and cook until al dente. Drain the pasta. Do not rinse. Then return pasta to the pot.

3.   Add the sauce to the pasta and gently toss to combine. Season with salt and pepper as you like. Divide among bowls and top with Parmigiano-Reggiano and a drizzle of extra-virgin olive oil.

OPTIONS: Use gluten-free pasta to make this dish gluten-free.

FRESH AND BRIGHT PASTA PRIMAVERA

Active time: 15 minutes | **Cook time:** 20 minutes | **Yield:** 4 servings

INGREDIENTS:

1 lb. whole-grain pasta

1 bunch fresh basil

1 cup low-sodium chicken stock

2 cloves garlic

2 tbsps extra-virgin olive oil

1 bunch green onions, chopped

1 tsp red pepper flakes

2 zucchinis, diced

1 cup sugar snap peas

½ cup shelled English peas

½ cup shelled edamame

1 bunch asparagus, stalks diced, tips left whole

½ cup Parmigiano-Reggiano, grated.

salt to taste

If you follow my recipe properly, you'll end up with a fresh and bright springtime garden on your plate. Here is my philosophy on cooking vegetables. Overcooking destroys vitamins and nutrients, and of course, taste. Meanwhile, it's okay to eat vegetables uncooked (See Grilled Corn & Summer Vegetable Salad on page 73). So I'm a big advocate of keeping vegetables bright, colorful, and fresh. They look yummy, taste amazing, and you get a full serving of nutritional goodness. This is a culinary no-brainer. Pasta Primavera is a simple dish. Pasta, fresh green vegetables, aromatics, and a touch of Parmigiano-Reggiano. It takes a few minutes to make, and it's delicious.

QUICK TIP: I know I keep repeating myself, but this is important information. The amount of time you cook pasta has an impact on fat loss. Overcooking boosts the glycemic index. For that reason (and because it tastes so good!), I recommend cooking pasta al dente, and even a couple of minutes less than what the manufacturer's package says. Cooked pasta should be slightly firm and offer some resistance when you chew it.

PREPARATION:

1. In a food processor, blend basil leaves, 1 tbsp of extra-virgin olive oil, and garlic together until smooth to make a quick pesto.

2. Heat 1 tbsp olive oil in a large saucepan over medium-high heat. Sauté zucchini, sugar snap peas, English peas, asparagus, edamame, and pepper flakes for 1 minute. Then add 1 cup of chicken stock and simmer for 3 minutes. You want to keep the vegetables as bright green as possible.

3. Pour the basil-garlic mixture into zucchini mixture. Remove from heat.

4. Meanwhile, bring a large pot of salted water to a boil. Add the pasta and cook until al dente. Drain the pasta. Do not rinse. Return to the pot.

5. Pour the sauce over pasta. Spread Parmigiano-Reggiano cheese on top. Serve hot.

....

OPTIONS: Use gluten-free pasta to make this dish gluten-free.

TRADITIONAL PASTA PUTTANESCA

Active time: 25 minutes | **Cook time:** 15 minutes | **Yield:** 4 servings

INGREDIENTS:

1 lb. whole-grain pasta

3 tbsps extra-virgin olive oil

3 cloves garlic, minced

2 cups canned San Marzano tomatoes, diced

4 anchovy filets, rinsed and chopped

2 tbsps tomato paste

3 tbsps capers

20 black olives, pitted and coarsely chopped

½ tsp crushed red pepper flakes

Pasta Puttanesca is a classic Italian pasta dish with a racy history, which will remain untold. We'll just leave it at the translation of "Puttanesca," which means "of the whore." Tomatoes, extra-virgin olive oil, capers, garlic, and olives are traditional to Southern Italy, where the dish originated.

QUICK TIP: Cook pasta al dente for faster fat loss and a classic Italian taste.

PREPARATION:

1. In a skillet over medium heat, heat up olive oil, add anchovies to dissolve, and brown garlic until golden. Add diced tomatoes and cook 5 minutes. Stir in tomato paste, capers, olives, and red pepper flakes. Cook 10 minutes, stirring occasionally.
2. Meanwhile, bring a large pot of salted water to a boil. Add the pasta and cook until al dente. Drain the pasta. Do not rinse. Return to the pot.
3. Pour the sauce over pasta. Serve hot.

OPTIONS: Use gluten-free pasta to make this dish gluten-free.

LEAN AND GREEN BAKED ZITI

Active time: 20 minutes | **Cook time:** 30 minutes | **Yield:** 4 servings

INGREDIENTS:

½ lb. whole grain ziti pasta

1 onion, chopped

3 cloves of garlic, minced

1 lb. 90% lean ground beef

2 medium cans San Marzano tomatoes, diced

6 ounces part skim mozzarella cheese, shredded

½ lb. of fresh spinach

¼ lb. of Swiss chard, stems removed

1 cup plain Greek yogurt

2 tbsps Parmigiano-Reggiano, grated

Baked ziti is a classic Italian-American dish. While it's not the best nutritional dish for fat loss, this recipe allows you to feed your hungry family, friends, and yourself on a budget. And it's still reasonable in terms of fat-burning nutrition, thanks to the use of whole-grain pasta, very limited fat, and the addition of a ton of leafy green vegetables.

QUICK TIP: You can assemble this ahead, and either refrigerate or freeze before you do the final baking. Or you can cook it and freeze it for later use.

PREPARATION:

1. Preheat the oven to 350° (175°c). In a large skillet, brown onion, garlic, and ground beef over medium heat. Add tomatoes and spinach and simmer 10 minutes.

2. Meanwhile, bring a large pot of salted water to a boil. Add the pasta and cook until al dente or rather, cook them about 2 minutes less than the manufacturer's recommendation for al dente pasta. Drain the pasta. Do not rinse. Return to the pot.

3. Mix pasta, mozzarella, tomatoes, and yogurt together, and place into a baking dish. Top with grated Parmesan cheese.

4. Bake for 20 minutes in the preheated oven, or until cheeses are melted.

OPTIONS: Use gluten-free pasta to make this dish gluten-free. Ziti obviously is used for this dish. But you can substitute penne pasta if you desire.

★ **FAV** ★

SPINACH AND RICOTTA LASAGNA

Active time: 25 minutes | **Cook time:** 55 minutes | **Yield:** 8 servings

INGREDIENTS:

12 ounces ground turkey

1 lb. of frozen spinach, thawed and squeezed dry

1 box of whole grain lasagna noodles

1 onion, minced

1 clove garlic, crushed

1 medium can San Marzano tomatoes, diced

2 tbsps tomato paste

1 sprig fresh basil, leaves torn

1 tsp dry oregano

6 ounces low-fat ricotta cheese

5 ounces part skim mozzarella cheese, sliced

5 ounces grated Parmesan cheese

salt and pepper to taste

There is lasagna, and then there is lasagna. Sure, you can grab a box of processed lasagna in the frozen section of your grocery store, and regret it down the road. Or you can quickly make your own, control what you put in your body, and have an awesome tasting experience. This lasagna recipe is one of our favorites. We love the taste, the amount of vegetables packed into it, and how easy it is to make.

QUICK TIP: Dark leafy greens such as spinach are important for skin and hair, bone health, and provide protein, iron, vitamins, and minerals such as potassium.

PREPARATION:

1. In a Dutch oven, cook turkey, onion, and garlic over medium heat until soft and cooked through. Stir in crushed tomatoes, tomato paste, tomato sauce. Season with basil, oregano, salt and pepper. Simmer covered for about 20 minutes, stirring occasionally.

2. In a mixing bowl, add the ricotta to the spinach and mix. Preheat oven to 375° (190°c).

3. To assemble, spread about 1 cup of meat sauce in the bottom of a baking dish. Arrange a few lasagna sheets over meat sauce. Spread with a thin layer of the ricotta mixture. Top with mozzarella cheese. Spoon another thin layer of sauce, and sprinkle some Parmesan cheese. Repeat layers, and top with remaining mozzarella and Parmesan cheese. Cover with foil.

4. Bake in preheated oven for 20 minutes. Remove foil, and bake an additional 15 minutes. Let it cool for a few minutes and serve.

LEAFY GREENS ENCHILADA

Active time: 20 minutes | **Cook time:** 50 minutes | **Yield:** 4 servings

INGREDIENTS:

1 quart of chopped kale and chard, steam off

1 cup canned or frozen corn

1½ cups part skim mozzarella, shredded

2 small cans chopped chipotle chilies

1 medium can diced tomatoes, diced

8 taco-sized whole-grain tortilla (such as Ezekiel's), warmed

4 cups white cabbage, thinly sliced

2 scallions, thinly sliced

¼ cup sunflower seeds

1 tbsp olive oil

juice of 1 lime

salt and pepper to taste

Meatless Monday? This is your new easy go-to recipe, and the best way to get your fix of fiber and vitamins A and C.

PREPARATION:

1. Preheat oven to 400° (200°c). In a medium skillet over medium-high heat, wilt the greens.
2. In a medium bowl, mix together the greens, corn, 1 cup of the mozzarellla and 1 can of the chilies. In another bowl, stir together to-matoes, the remaining can of chilies, salt and pepper to taste.
3. Dividing evenly, roll up the greens mixture in the tortillas. Place seam-side down in a shallow baking dish. Top with the tomato sauce and the remaining mozzarella. Cover with foil and bake until bubbling, about 20 minutes. Uncover and bake until golden, about 10 minutes more.
4. Meanwhile, in a large bowl, toss the cabbage and scallions with the sunflower seeds, oil, and lime juice. Salt and pepper to taste. Serve with the enchiladas.

SERVING INFO: 220 calories, 25g fat, 5g carbohydrates, 22g protein, 2g fiber, 0g sugar

NO-BREAD GRILLED CHEESE SANDWICH

Active time: 20 minutes | **Cook time:** 30 minutes | **Yield:** 4 servings

INGREDIENTS:

1 large broccoli head, cut into florets

2 ounces part skim mozzarella cheese, shredded

2 ounces grated Parmigiano-Reggiano, grated.

1 egg, lightly beaten

2 egg whites, lightly beaten

1 tbsp of olive oil

5 oz. aged cheddar cheese, sliced

salt and pepper to taste

When you daydream about your childhood, a few of your memories probably involve a gooey grilled cheese sandwich. Yet, most of us try to limit our carb intake and/or gluten, and sometimes we need a bread recipe without bread. Here is a secret way to make grilled cheese healthier.

I didn't come up with this bright idea. Apparently, there is a cauliflower crust craze in the trendy places of America. I wasn't aware and didn't even know, despite my 23 years of culinary experience, about the cauliflower crust craze. However, it sounded intriguing so I decided to give it a try. While experimenting in the kitchen, I wondered if I could do the same thing with broccoli since it is similar to cauliflower and comes from the same botanical family. The two are also almost identical in texture and taste.

Here is your secret way to make grilled cheese much healthier.

FOR THE BREADLESS 'BREAD'

1. Preheat oven to 450° (230°c). In a food processor, pulse the broccoli until it looks like uncooked grits or couscous. Heat the olive oil in a skillet over medium heat. Cook the 3 cups of the broccoli, and sauté for 10 minutes to soften and dry out. Do not brown.

2. Set aside the broccoli in a mixing bowl. Add egg, Parmigiano-Reggiano, mozzarella, salt and pepper, and mix well. Using your hands, shape 8 balls, and transfer to a baking sheet lined with parchment paper. Flatten the balls to shape 8 pieces resembling bread slices. Bake in the oven for about 12 to 15 minutes.

TO ASSEMBLE:

1. As soon as the 'bread' slices come out of the oven and are still warm, cover them liberally with cheese, and top with the remaining slice of broccoli bread. Serve at once.

FAT-BURNING PIZZA

Active time: 20 minutes | **Cook time:** 35 minutes | **Yield:** 4 servings

INGREDIENTS:

¼ cup coconut flour

¼ cup whole grain flour

2 eggs

2 tsps baking powder

1 cup low-fat milk

1 tsp garlic powder

salt and pepper to taste

Chicago deep-dish, New-York style, Neapolitan pizza, California style. Let me now introduce you to the fat-burning pizza. Just check out the list of ingredients and be amazed: no refined flour, no or very little fat.

QUICK TIP: This recipe is for the crust only. Then you can garnish with your toppings of choice. A thin layer of San Marzano tomatoes, topped with fresh basil and a dusting of Parmesan cheese is a good start. What about fresh spinach, maybe even some kale or Swiss chard? Some lean chicken breast would make a nice addition, as well as mushrooms and other assorted vegetables.

PREPARATION:

1. Preheat oven to 375° (190°c). Whisk all ingredients in a bowl. Rest the dough for a few minutes.
2. On a baking sheet lined with parchment paper, spread the batter with a rolling pin, shaping it like a pizza crust.
3. Bake at 375° (190°c) for 25-30 minutes until slightly golden brown.
4. Put sauce, cheese, and toppings on and cook for an additional 10 minutes until cheese is melted. Serve hot.

CRISPY SWEET POTATO FRIES

Active time: 15 minutes | **Cook time:** 25 minutes | **Yield:** 4 servings

INGREDIENTS:

4 large sweet potatoes, peeled and cut into ¼-inch-thick wedges

2 tbsps cornstarch

2 tbsps extra-virgin olive oil

a pinch of cayenne pepper

1 tsp paprika or cumin or curry powder

2 garlic cloves, minced

4 sprigs of Italian parsley, chopped

salt and pepper to taste

I was 26 years old the first time I saw sweet potatoes. They're not common in France where I grew up. Since tasting them, however, I've become addicted. Not only because they are sweet, delicious, and cook very quickly, but they also provide a healthier replacement for plain ol' potatoes. These sweet potato fries are low in starch, a much better option than French fries and there is no frying involved. Baking sweet potato 'fries' at the right temperature makes the difference. One more thing. We're talking sweet potatoes here, not yams. I know they look similar, but sweet potatoes are more nutritious.

QUICK TIP: Your challenge is to 'crisp' *the* sweet potato fries just enough to avoid burning them. It may take a couple of tries in your oven to suit your taste. If you can time this right and control your oven, you may get away without the cornstarch, which is only included to help with the crust. Have fun and experiment!

PREPARATION:

1. Preheat the oven to 425° (220°c). Peel the sweet potatoes and cut them uniformly into long wedges so the fries bake evenly.
2. In a re-sealable plastic bag, sprinkle the uncooked fries with cornstarch and then pour just enough extra-virgin olive oil to lightly coat the fries. Season with salt, pepper, garlic, and spices. Mix to distribute evenly.
3. Pour the fries directly onto a non-stick baking sheet in a single layer so they have a chance to crisp up.
4. Bake for 25 minutes, or until the fries are crispy. Make sure you wait long enough for the fries to crisp, or they will turn out soft.
5. Serve with sprinkled chopped parsley.

HEARTY YELLOW SQUASH CASSEROLE

Active time: 20 minutes | **Cook time:** 30 minutes | **Yield:** 4 servings

INGREDIENTS:

4 cups yellow squash, sliced

½ cup onion, chopped

½ cup whole grain, unsweetened cereals (such as Ezekiel), processed into crumbs

½ cup shredded part skim mozzarella cheese

3 egg whites, beaten

¼ cup low-fat milk

3 tbsps extra-virgin olive oil

pinch of cayenne pepper

salt and pepper to taste

You should hear the heated discussion at our family dinner table! Is yellow squash a fruit, or is it a vegetable? My eldest son Julian vehemently argues (and rightly so!) that it's a fruit. In my deepest paternal voice and with the full extent of my culinary knowledge, I recite all the desserts one cannot make with yellow squash: "Would you eat yellow squash crème brulee? Yellow squash shortcake? Yellow squash foster? Yellow squash upside-down pie? Red velvet yellow squash cake maybe?"

Regardless of its botanical origin, yellow squash is another family favorite. And this particular recipe is a winner. It is satisfying as a homemade casserole, healthy like a vegetable (or a fruit, I suppose!), and easy to make. The recipe is perfect.

QUICK TIP: Instead of breadcrumbs, I use whole-grain, unsweetened cereals that I pulse for a few seconds in a food processor. This easy and nutritious 'breadcrumb substitute' adds crunch to any casserole.

PREPARATION:

1. Preheat oven to 400° (200°c).
2. Place squash and onion in a large skillet over medium heat. Pour in a small amount of water. Cover, and cook until squash is tender, about 5 minutes. Drain well, and place in a large bowl.
3. Add half of the crumbs to the squash and onion mixture.
4. Mix eggs and milk together. Then add to the squash and onion mixture. Season with salt, pepper and cayenne pepper. Pour into an ovenproof dish. Top with mozzarella cheese. Sprinkle with remaining 'breadcrumbs' and drizzle with extra-virgin olive oil.
5. Bake in preheated oven for 25 minutes, or until lightly browned.

ROASTED FAUX FRIES

Active time: 10 minutes | **Cook time:** 30 minutes | **Yield:** 4 servings

INGREDIENTS:

2 lbs. rutabaga

2 tbsps cornstarch

2 tbsps extra-virgin olive oil

3 cloves garlic, minced

2 tbsps fresh Italian parsley, minced

1 pinch of cayenne pepper

salt and pepper to taste

Rutabaga is the 'great unknown' vegetable! It is readily available in most grocery stores. When cooked, rutabaga looks and feels exactly like potatoes, but tastes better. In fact, many of my clients get fooled. I often hear, "What did you do to these potatoes? They're great." You too, can make fake roasted potatoes for your loved ones, as well as give them the delicious gift of good nutrition—all from a rutabaga.

QUICK TIP: The skin of a rutabaga is somewhat thick and waxy. The best way to safely peel it is to cut off the top and bottom so it stands steadily on your cutting board. Then, using a large knife (and your hands away from that large knife), cut off the skin around the rutabaga, working your way down.

PREPARATION:

1. Preheat the oven to 425° (220°c).
2. Peel and cut the rutabaga into the size of fries. In a re-sealable plastic bag, sprinkle the uncooked fries with cornstarch and then pour enough olive oil to lightly coat them. Season with salt, pepper, cayenne, and garlic. Mix to distribute evenly.
3. Transfer the fries to a sheet pan and spread out into a single layer.
4. Roast in the oven for 30 minutes or until browned and crisp. Flip twice with a spatula during cooking in order to ensure even browning.
5. Remove the rutabaga fries from the oven, toss with parsley, adjust seasoning, and serve hot.

10-MINUTE TIMESAVER: Use your oven's convection setting, if you have one. It cooks twenty percent faster and saves your precious time and money on your electrical bill. Adapt the cooking time accordingly when you use this chef's secret.

OPTIONS: The cornstarch is optional. It just helps with the 'crisping.'

ZUCCHINI AU GRATIN

Active time: 10 minutes | **Cook time:** 30 minutes | **Yield:** 4 servings

INGREDIENTS:

4 zucchini sliced ¼-inch thick crosswise

4 tbsps extra-virgin olive oil

3 yellow onions, sliced

1 tsp ground nutmeg

4 tbsps coconut flour

1 cup milk

⅓ cup whole-grain, unsweetened cereals (such as Ezekiel's), processed into crumbs

½ cup grated part-skim mozzarella

1 tsp paprika

a pinch of cayenne pepper

salt and pepper to taste

When you grow up around the Mediterranean Sea, as I did, you know zucchini. In fact, you know too much! As summer approaches and weather gets warm and sunny, all Mediterranean vegetables blossom at once, and become plentiful. They pop up everywhere. Families cook them en masse, and they appear in various ways, often twice or three times in the same menu. Consider fried zucchini fritters, zucchini in ratatouille, in minestrone, zucchini bread, and one of my favorites—zucchini au gratin.

This recipe is absolutely delicious and will become a favorite!

QUICK TIP: Variations in oven temperatures occur. Rely on your senses. We want a beautiful, bubbly, golden and crusty top. Monitor the look of your casserole to perfection.

PREPARATION:

1. Preheat the oven to 400° (200°c).
2. In a very large sauté pan, add the olive oil, and cook the onions over medium-high heat for about 20 minutes, or until tender but not browned.
3. Add the zucchini and cook covered for 10 minutes or until tender. Add the salt, pepper, and nutmeg and cook uncovered for 5 more minutes. Stir in the flour. Add the hot milk and cook over low heat for a few minutes, until it makes a sauce. Pour the mixture into an ovenproof dish, and sprinkle with the reserved 'breadcrumbs.' Top with mozzarella.
4. Bake for 20 minutes, or until bubbly and browned.

10-MINUTE TIMESAVER:

Use your oven's convection setting, if you have one. It cooks twenty percent fast-

er and saves your precious time and money on your electric bill. Adapt the cooking time accordingly when you use this chef's secret.

OPTIONS:
1. Use gluten-free breadcrumbs if you are on a gluten-free diet.
2. To add variety, replace some of the zucchini with eggplant or yellow squash.
3. Add garlic, cayenne, and fresh herbs such as basil, lots of it, to spice things up a bit.

NFO: 320 cal

ROASTED BUTTERNUT SQUASH AND HAZELNUT

Active time: 15 minutes | **Cook time:** 25 minutes | **Yield:** 4 servings

INGREDIENTS:

1 large butternut squash, peeled and cubed

2 tbsps extra-virgin olive oil

2 tbsps garlic, minced

2 tbsps basil, chopped

½ cup hazelnuts, toasted, and roughly chopped

1 tbsp lemon juice

1 tbsp minced fresh chives

salt and pepper to taste

I am reminded of famed Spanish chef Jose Andres who, far from being a vegetarian, often promotes vegetables as a tastier option to meat. He says the taste of a vegetable lingers in your mouth. I agree with him. Chew on a piece of cooked chicken and after a bite or two, the flavor is gone. But the taste of roasted butternut squash will delight your taste buds for a much longer time.

Simplicity and wholesome ingredients are often the way to go in the kitchen. Roasting butternut squash is so simple, quick and easy, and results in a deliciously moist and tender flesh with caramelized edges.

QUICK TIP: Cut off the top and bottom so it stands steadily on your cutting board. Then, using a large knife (and your hands away from that large knife), cut off the skin around the squash, working your way down.

PREPARATION:

1. Preheat oven to 425° (220°c) degrees. Toss squash with extra-virgin olive oil, garlic, basil, salt and pepper until evenly coated. Arrange squash on baking sheet in a single layer. Roast squash until most of it is well browned, and tender, about 25 minutes.
2. Meanwhile, toast hazelnuts on a baking sheet for about 10 minutes in the oven or until they become really fragrant. Remove from oven.
3. Transfer squash to a serving platter. Sprinkle hazelnuts, chives, and lemon juice over squash, and serve at once.

10-MINUTE TIMESAVER: Use your oven's convection setting, if you have one. It cooks twenty percent faster and saves your precious time and money on your electrical bill. Adapt the cooking time accordingly when you use this chef's secret.

OPTIONS:

1. Any nuts will work: cashew, Brazil nuts, walnuts or pecans. Have fun experimenting!
2. Most fresh herbs work well too: fresh thyme, oregano, tarragon

RAINBOW ROOT VEGETABLE ROAST

Active time: 25 minutes | **Cook time:** 30 minutes | **Yield:** 4 servings

INGREDIENTS:

1 rutabaga, peeled and cubed

2 beets, peeled and cubed

4 carrots, unpeeled and sliced

1 parsnip, unpeeled and sliced

2 turnips, unpeeled and cubed

¼ cup minced fresh rosemary or thyme

3 tbsps extra-virgin olive oil

6 cloves garlic, minced

1 tsp paprika

1 tsp cumin

½ tsp cayenne pepper

salt and pepper to taste

Most root vegetables are available year-round. But when fall comes and leaves are changing, when it's a little chillier and pumpkins and squash start populating markets, it's time to indulge and cook rutabaga, beets, carrots, parsnips and celery root. We leave summer behind and enjoy the autumn mood that fills the air. Root vegetables are excellent. They fill you up like carbs do, yet generally have a low glycemic index, and are packed with antioxidants, fiber, vitamins C, B, A, and iron too.

QUICK TIP: Make sure you use plastic gloves to handle the beets, or they will leave stains on your fingers.

PREPARATION:

1. Preheat oven to 400° (200°c). Combine all vegetables in a large baking dish.
2. Mix rosemary/thyme, olive oil, garlic, and sea salt in a small bowl; pour over vegetables and toss to coat.
3. Bake, covered, for 20 minutes. Uncover and bake until vegetables are tender, about another 15 minutes.

10-MINUTE TIMESAVER: Use your oven's convection setting, if you have one. It cooks twenty percent faster and saves your precious time and money on your electrical bill. Adapt the cooking time accordingly when you use this chef's secret.

OPTIONS: Mix up the vegetables, substituting any root veggie such as celery root, jicama, and even sweet potatoes or butternut squash

NOT-SO-FRENCH FRIES

Active time: 15 minutes | **Cook time:** 25 minutes | **Yield:** 4 servings

INGREDIENTS:

2 lbs. parsnips, unpeeled and cut into 2½-inch-long fingers

4 tsps extra virgin olive oil, divided in 2

½ cup dry white wine

1 tbsp prepared horseradish

1 tbsp fresh Italian parsley, chopped

1 tbsp fresh chives, chopped

1 tbsp poppy seeds

salt and pepper to taste

Parsnips look like white carrots and are full of minerals, vitamins, and antioxidants. They have a rich and sweet flavor. They also pair very well with horseradish and Italian parsley, which is actually a close cousin.

QUICK TIP: Keep parsnips unpeeled. A lot of the taste and vitamins lay just beneath the skin, and removing it with a peeler would be a tragedy!

PREPARATION:

1. Preheat the oven to 375˚ (190˚c).
2. Toss the parsnips with 2 teaspoons olive oil and salt and pepper to taste. Add the parsnips and the wine in an ovenproof dish. Bake until the parsnips are tender and the wine has been absorbed, about 25 minutes.
3. When the parsnips are cooked, mix with horseradish, parsley, chives, and poppy seeds, and season with salt and pepper.
4. Serve immediately.

10-MINUTE TIMESAVER: Use your oven's convection setting. It cooks twenty percent faster and saves your precious time and money on your electrical bill. Adapt the cooking time accordingly when you use this chef's secret.

OPTIONS:

1. Put carrots into the mix and add variety.
2. Replace poppy seeds with sesame or flax seeds, if desired.

BEAT THE BEETROOT

Active time: 10 minutes | **Cook time:** 1 hour | **Yield:** 4 servings

INGREDIENTS:

4 lbs. red beets, skin on, scrubbed, halved if large

2 tbsps extra-virgin olive oil

chopped herbs such as thyme, rosemary, sage, parsley and/or basil.

1 tsp prepare horseradish

4 tbsps of shelled pistachios, toasted

4 cloves of garlic, minced

½ cup of crumbled Feta cheese

salt and pepper to taste

You either love or hate beets. That's just the way it is. If you're a beet hater, canned cooked beets are probably what turned you off at some point. Who can blame you?

But because millions of beet lovers can't all be wrong, you owe it to yourself to give beets a chance. And today, here is your opportunity. I'm a beet lover. I throw them in soups to make Russian Borscht. I roast them, grill them, steam them, make red-violet aioli or mashed potatoes. I even feed them to my kids' schoolmates when I visit their school during the Great American Teach-In each year. This roasted beet recipe is beet 101. Roasted, they lose moisture and become a tad bit more flavorful. Paired with thyme, feta cheese, and nuts, they take on a gourmet dimension of their own and reveal their full potential. Then we're back to square one. You either love 'em or hate 'em.

QUICK TIP: Use plastic gloves to cut beets or you'll end up with purple fingers.

PREPARATION:

1. Preheat oven to 400° (200°c). Toss beets with oil in an ovenproof baking dish; season with salt and pepper. Add garlic, horseradish, the herbs and ¼ cup water. Cover pan tightly with foil so the steam stays around the beets.
2. Roast beets until a paring knife slips easily through flesh, about 60 minutes. Remove from oven. Sprinkle crumbled feta and toasted pistachios. Serve hot or chilled.

TIMESAVER: Beets can be roasted ahead of time and then served cold in a salad.

OPTIONS: Enjoy variations of this recipe by substituting pistachios for other nuts, and feta cheese for some other cheese.

MAC AND CHEESE AND KALE

Active time: 25 minutes | **Cook time:** 30 minutes | **Yield:** 4 servings

INGREDIENTS:

4 tbsps whole-grain, unsweetened cereals (such as Ezekiel), processed into crumbs

3 tbsps extra-virgin olive oil

2 scallions, thinly sliced

2 garlic cloves, minced

4 tbsps coconut flour

3 cups fat-free milk

4 slices smoked Gouda cheese

2 tbsps grated fresh Parmesan cheese

3 cups coarsely chopped kale

2 cups whole grain elbow macaroni, cooked al dente

1 tsp paprika
a pinch of cayenne pepper

1 tsp nutmeg

salt and pepper to taste

Find me a kid who doesn't like mac and cheese. Actually, find me an adult who doesn't like mac and cheese. This classic dish has been updated with slight smoky flavors, and the sneaky addition of kale, which provides an alternative flavor, fiber, and nutrients. My children all love mac and cheese. And they absolutely love this version. If only they knew about the kale!

QUICK TIP: I know mac and cheese is a classic dish that purists fiercely protect. Yet, to make it fun, try other cheeses, add vegetables, and spices. Nutmeg, for instance, works very well with it.

PREPARATION:

1. Preheat oven to 350° (180°c). Pour olive oil in a large saucepan over medium heat. Add scallions and garlic; cook 1 minute.
2. Add coconut flour; cook 1 minute, stirring constantly. Gradually add milk, salt, pepper, cayenne, paprika and nutmeg, stirring constantly with a whisk until blended.
3. Bring to a simmer; cook until slightly thicker (about 2 minutes). Take off the heat, and add cheeses and stir until melted.
4. Add kale and cooked pasta to cheese sauce, stirring until well blended. Spoon mixture into an ovenproof baking dish. Sprinkle with 'breadcrumbs.'
5. Bake at 350° (180°c) for 15 minutes or until lightly brown on top, and bubbly.

25-MINUTE TIMESAVER: Another awesome make ahead! Prepare this recipe a few hours or even the day

before, and leave step 5 for dinnertime. If you do, please increase the ratio of sauce vs. pasta, or the pasta will end up absorbing most of the sauce, and dry things out.

OPTIONS: In this recipe, you can replace kale with spinach or any leafy greens. You can also substitute cheeses, too. Try part-skim mozzarella, romano, or ricotta. I use whole-grain rotini pasta because my kids love it. But feel free to play with the shape of pasta. For a gluten-free dish, simply switch to gluten-free pasta.

SERVING INFO: 380 calories, 17g fat, 43g carbohydrates, 18g protein, 9g fiber, 18g sugar

GREEN BEAN CASSEROLE

Active time: 15 minutes | **Cook time:** 30 minutes | **Yield:** 4 servings

INGREDIENTS:

1 tbsp extra-virgin olive oil

1 tbsp buckwheat flour

½ onion, diced

1 cup plain Greek yogurt

1 lb. fresh green beans

1 cup shredded part skim mozzarella

¼ cup whole-grain, unsweetened cereals (such as Ezekiel's), processed into crumbs

salt and pepper to taste

Green bean casserole is such an important feature of American culture. In the 1950s, there were two items most Americans always had on hand––green beans and a can of Campbell's Cream of Mushroom Soup. And that's how green bean casserole was created and became a staple at the Thanksgiving table. I have tweaked my green bean recipe, adapting it for fitness. I hope it will now become a staple on your Thanksgiving table. Enjoy!

PREPARATION:

1. Preheat oven to 350° (175°c).
2. In a large pot of boiling water, or in a steamer, cook the beans until softer and brighter, about 6 minutes. Drain the water and reserve the beans.
3. Pour 2 tbsps extra-virgin olive oil in a large skillet over medium heat. Stir in flour until smooth, to make a roux, and cook for one minute. Salt and pepper to taste. Add onion, yogurt, and green beans, and stir to coat.
4. Transfer the mixture to an ovenproof baking dish. Sprinkle cheese and 'breadcrumbs' over the top.
5. Bake for 20 minutes in the preheated oven, or until the top is golden and cheese is bubbly.

5-MINUTE TIMESAVER: Use your oven's convection setting, if you have one. It cooks twenty percent faster and saves your precious time and money on your electrical bill. Adapt the cooking time accordingly when you use this chef's secret.

CARAMELIZED BRUSSELS SPROUTS

Active time: 10 minutes | **Cook time:** 25 minutes | **Yield:** 4 servings

INGREDIENTS:

3 tbsps extra-virgin olive oil

4 cups fresh Brussels sprouts, halved lengthwise

1 onion, diced

2 tbsps sesame seeds

salt and pepper to taste

I feel bad for Brussels sprouts, the tiny vegetable with a bad rep. People complain about their smell and how much they dislike 'em. Life must be hard for this poor little veggie.

Chances are, though, if you dislike (or hate!) Brussels sprouts, it's because you have no idea how to cook them. Granted, overcooking will turn them brownish, mushy, and very smelly. Instead we want bright green vegetables, a nice sear, firm to the tooth, tasty but not offensively tasty, nice and subtle. Brussels sprouts are about subtlety of taste and texture. And that's what you get if you simply cut the buds off, maybe in half, and then sauté them in olive oil. Add a little salt and pepper, and voila! Give the sprouts a chance.

PREPARATION:

1. In a skillet over medium-high heat, add sesame seeds and toast for about 3 minutes, or until golden brown and fragrant. Reserve.
2. In the same pan over medium-high heat, slightly brown onions with 2 tbsps of olive oil, until they are soft, about 10 minutes. Reserve.
3. Add 1 more tbsp of olive oil to the hot skillet and add Brussels sprouts. Brown and caramelize them in the pan without stirring much. After 10 minutes, add the onions back, and the sesame seeds.
4. Serve hot on a plate and season with coarse sea salt.

KIDS' FAV KALE CHIPS

Active time: 10 minutes | **Cook time:** 10 minutes | **Yield:** 4 servings

INGREDIENTS:

1 large bunch of kale

2 tsps extra-virgin olive oil

1 tsp salt

Kale leaves crisp like magic in the oven. If there is only one vegetable your kids will eat, this is it. No question about it. This is a favorite among all the kids I cook for. It's also a fast and easy recipe that I came up with a couple of years ago when I had the opportunity to prepare a wine dinner with celebrity chef Tyler Florence. We casually spent four or five hours preparing food at my client's residence. I got to meet, cook with, and chitchat with Tyler. He made his famous fried chicken (really a great twist on the Southern classic) and also some kale chips. I didn't know at the time that kale 'crisps' so well in the oven.

QUICK TIP: It's critical to place the kale in a single layer without crowding. Then bake so it is evenly exposed to heat and dehydrates to a crisp.

PREPARATION:

1. Preheat an oven to 375˚ (190˚c).
2. Remove the leaves from the thick stems and tear into bite size pieces. Wash and thoroughly dry kale using a salad spinner and paper towels. It's very important that no water remains.
3. Drizzle kale with olive oil, sprinkle with salt, and toss. Then lay on baking sheets in one single layer.
4. Bake until the edges brown but are not burnt, about 15 minutes.

SERVING INFO: 120 calories, 7g fat, 13g carbohydrates, 6g protein, 5g fiber, 4g sugar

WILTED BLACK KALE WITH COCONUT

Active time: 3 minutes | **Cook time:** 3 minutes | **Yield:** 4 servings

INGREDIENTS:

8 cups lacinato, black, or curly kale, stemmed

1 seeded jalapeno pepper, minced

2 tsps of extra-virgin olive oil

2 tbsps light coconut milk

3 tbsps unsweetened coconut flakes

Also called lacinato kale, black kale is a traditional staple of Tuscan cuisine. It's easy to prepare and cook. Strangely enough, black kale, spinach, and most leafy greens pair beautifully with coconut. That combination is found abundantly in Indian cuisine, for instance. This is an exciting way to add a superfood to your diet.

QUICK TIP: Wilting is simply exposing leafy greens to heat for a few seconds—just enough so they lose their spring and get a nice bright green color. Don't be afraid to undercook greens.

PREPARATION:

1. Heat a skillet over medium-high heat and add oil. If using, sauté the jalapeno for a few seconds. Add the kale and wilt for a few more seconds.
2. Add coconut milk. Continue cooking for 2 minutes.
3. Transfer the kale to a plate, sprinkle with coconut flakes, and serve hot.

OPTIONS: Instead of black kale, you can use curly kale, chard, beetroot leaves, or spinach.

BROCCOLI AND SPINACH CASSEROLE

Active time: 10 minutes | **Cook time:** 30 minutes | **Yield:** 4 servings

INGREDIENTS:

2 heads of broccoli, chopped

1 box frozen chopped spinach, thawed

6 ounces shredded part skim mozzarella

1 onion, chopped

2 cups plain Greek yogurt

1 egg

2 egg whites

1 tbsp extra-virgin olive oil

½ cup whole grain, unsweetened cereals (such as Ezekiel's), processed into crumbs

1 tbsp paprika

½ tsp of cayenne pepper

salt and pepper to taste

Broccoli and spinach surely bring intense childhood memories. Without Popeye and Olive Oil, none of us would have eaten spinach. Broccoli wasn't served much in my hometown in the south of France, and I can't recall eating it before I started working as a chef in England fresh out of chef school. There I learned to cook it the way the British taught me––steamed a few seconds till it turns neon green. This broccoli and spinach casserole couldn't be easier. A mere 10-minute prep will send you on your way to dinner heaven.

QUICK TIP: You can use fresh spinach if you prefer, but you'll have to wilt the leaves briefly in a hot pan before use. You can also substitute other leafy greens.

PREPARATION:

1. Preheat oven to 325° (160°c).
2. Mix all the ingredients together except the olive oil and the crumbs, and pour into an ovenproof dish.
3. Mix the crumbs with the olive oil. Sprinkle the crumbs on top of the broccoli mixture and bake for 30 minutes.

TIMESAVER: Use your oven's convection setting, if you have one. It cooks twenty percent faster and saves your precious time and money on your electrical bill. Adapt the cooking time accordingly when you use this chef's secret.

OPTIONS: Don't hesitate to change the ratio of broccoli to spinach.

HARD-BOILED EGGS

Active time: Less than 5 minutes | **Cook time:** 7½ minutes | **Yield:** 4 servings

INGREDIENTS:

4 eggs

1 tbsp vinegar

You may think that hard boiling eggs is as easy as boiling water. It's not. Disasters may occur. Eggs can break, undercook, overcook, smell like sulphur, develop a green ring around the yolk, and they can be a nightmare to peel. And depending on your altitude, pass-or-fail variations may surprise you.

I've known how to hard boil eggs since I was sixteen. Or so I thought. Then I met someone with real skill. The Grand Master of hard-boiled eggs, the hard-boiled egg chef of all is my wife Carissa.

This is her recipe. Follow it and you will never fail. Beautiful, perfect hard-boiled eggs. Every time.

QUICK TIP: Adding vinegar to the water helps keep egg whites from running out if an egg cracks while cooking. Do not salt the water.

PREPARATION:

1. Bring water and vinegar to a full rolling boil, in a saucepan over medium-high heat.
2. Add eggs carefully with a slotted spoon.
3. Time 7½ minutes. Remove eggs from the water with a slotted spoon, and put in a bowl. Let the eggs cool at room temperature, then refrigerate.

TOASTED BRAZIL NUTS

Active time: Less than 5 minutes | **Cook time:** 10 minutes | **Yield:** 8 servings

INGREDIENTS:

12 oz. Brazil nuts

A Brazilian friend once told me that it is illegal in his country to cut down a Brazil nut tree, despite the fact that the nut and its shell, heavy and rigid, is a hazard to vehicles and persons passing under the tree. In addition, the fruit is so dense that it sinks in fresh water and causes clogged waterways. Despite this hazard to Brazil, we're glad to have Brazil nuts here. They are an excellent source of protein, fiber, and vitamins. But most of all they're so good! Fat and meaty, crunchy and soft at the same time, they have great flavor.

QUICK TIP: All nuts benefit from a gentle toasting, which intensifies the flavor and maximizes their crunchiness.

PREPARATION:

1. Preheat oven to 350° (180°c). Spread Brazil nuts in a single layer on a baking sheet.
2. The nuts will be ready in about 10 minutes. You'll know they're done when they're lightly browned and that nutty smell fills the air.

SERVING INFO: 340 calories, 16g fat, 23g carbohydrates, 2g protein, 5g fiber, 12g sugar

STRAWBERRY AND CHOCOLATE

Active time: 5 minutes | **Cook time:** Less that 5 minutes | **Yield:** 4 servings

INGREDIENTS:

2 cups of fresh strawberries

1 cup dark chocolate (85-99% cocoa)

½ cup coconut milk

½ tsp vanilla extract

You may have thought that chocolate was out of reach if you want to stay fit. Not true. Dark chocolate can improve your health and lower the risk of heart disease. It's also a powerful source of antioxidants. Sure, commercial chocolate is loaded with sugar and should be avoided. But dark chocolate that is minimally processed and contains over 70% of cocoa (ideally 85% to 99%), is high in fiber and has a low glycemic index.

Let me introduce you to chocolate *ganache*, a fun French word, which means chocolate and cream. We chefs use ganache all the time to make chocolate sauce, to glaze a cake, or whip a mousse. Ganache softens chocolate and turns it into a rich dip. It's easy to make and convenient. The one problem is cream. So I replace the cream with coconut milk and it works wonders.

PREPARATION:
1. Place the coarsely chopped dark chocolate in a blender glass attachment.
2. Heat up the coconut milk in the microwave until it steams.
3. Pour the hot coconut milk over the chopped chocolate and let stand without stirring for 5 minutes. After 5 minutes, put the lid on the attachment, and blend until glossy and smooth. Add the vanilla extract and stir until incorporated. Serve warm or slightly cooled with fresh strawberries.

G INFO: 260

EASY GRANOLA BAR

Active time: 25 minutes | **Cook time:** N/A | **Yield:** 10 bars

INGREDIENTS:

1 cup Medjool dates, pitted

¼ cup honey

¼ cup natural almond butter

1 cup roasted unsalted almonds

1 cup rolled oats

½ cup dried cranberries

Why buy sugar-loaded snack bars when it's so easy to make your own? This recipe requires no baking, and is completed in less than 25 minutes.

It's a no-brainer recipe. And the bars are very tasty.

QUICK TIP: Make several batches of this recipe and keep the bars in resealable plastic bags in your refrigerator for a week or two.

PREPARATION:

1. Preheat oven at 350˚ (180˚c). Pulse dates in a food processor until texture is grainy and it forms a ball around the blade.
2. Toast oats and almonds in the oven for 10 minutes.
3. In a bowl, mix together oats, almonds, cranberries, and dates.
4. Add honey and almond butter into the oat mixture and mix.
5. Transfer to a rectangular pan lined up with parchment paper. Press down until uniformly flattened. Refrigerate for 20 minutes.
6. Remove granola from pan and slice into even bars. Store in an airtight container for up to 7 days.

SERVING INFO: 240 calories, 10g fat, 33g carbohydrates, 9g protein, 9g fiber, 8g sugar

CARROTS AND HOMEMADE HUMMUS

Active time: 5 minutes | **Cook time:** N/A | **Yield:** 2.5 cups

INGREDIENTS:

4 carrots, washed and cut into strips

1 small can garbanzo beans

4 tbsps lemon juice

2 tbsps tahini (sesame seed paste)

2 cloves garlic, minced

1 tbsps extra-virgin olive oil

salt and pepper to taste

Sure, you can buy hummus at the grocery store. Various kinds are everywhere. But come on, it is so easy and quick to make (and much better tasting!) that you can't pass on this. And keep in mind you can customize ingredients to your precise liking.

QUICK TIP: Garbanzo beans are the basic ingredient. But you can replace them with other beans for some variety. Try cannellini, pinto, navy, and others.

PREPARATION:

1. In a food processor, pulse half of the garbanzo beans, tahini, lemon juice, olive oil, minced garlic, salt and pepper.
2. Add the other half of the garbanzo beans to the food processor, then process for 1 minute more, until thick and smooth. Add cold water if necessary to achieve the consistency you want.
3. Scrape the hummus into a bowl and sprinkle with paprika.
4. Arrange carrots around it.

MAKE-YOUR-OWN JERKY

Active time: 20 minutes (plus marinating time) | **Cook time:** 4 hours | **Yield:** 4 servings

INGREDIENTS:

1 lb. flank steak

3 tbsps Worcestershire sauce

3 tbsps soy sauce

1 tbsp honey

1 tsp freshly ground black pepper

1 tsp onion powder

1 tsp liquid smoke

1 tsp red pepper flakes

Jerky is a prime example of something you should make yourself—and it's fun. Heavily processed, store-bought jerky contains large amounts of sodium and nitrite. Reproducing a century-old Native American process is cool. Prior to the invention of refrigeration, jerky allowed humans to both store food for long periods of time and have an easily carried source of nutrition when traveling.

QUICK TIP: Keep in mind that the jerky will firm up as it cools. It's ready when it is dry and dark in color.

PREPARATION:

1. Slice the meat, with the grain, into long thin strips.
2. Mix all ingredients in a resealable plastic bag. Add the meat and marinate overnight in the refrigerator.
3. Preheat oven to 175° (80°c) or its minimum setting. Remove the strips and pat dry.
4. Remove and spray the oven racks with nonstick cooking spray. Arrange the meat strips side-by-side across the racks, leaving some space between them.
5. Place the racks of meat in the oven and cook until completely dry, about 4 hours. Store in an airtight container for several weeks.

SERVING INFO: 180 calories, 15g fat, 9g carbohydrates, 6g protein, 7g fiber, 1g sugar

COTTAGE CHEESE-STUFFED AVOCADO

Active time: 5 minutes | **Cook time:** N/A | **Yield:** 4 servings

INGREDIENTS:

2 avocados

8 tbsps of low-fat cottage cheese

You don't even need to bother with dirtying a dish. This is a no-cook, superfast recipe that will get you out on the road quickly. Your only challenge will be finding perfect avocados. They often appear in stores either overripe or underripe. The ideal avocado is plump and brown, not green. Feel it and make sure it is full and gives a little when pressed.

QUICK TIP: Feel free to experiment with herbs and spices. Add curry powder, cayenne pepper or paprika. Add fresh dill, mint, or basil.

PREPARATION:
1. Cut avocados in half. Remove pits.
2. Fill the holes with two tbsps of low-fat cottage cheese in each avocado.
3. To serve, use a spoon to scoop bites right out of the avocado rind.

SERVING INFO: 180 calories, 7g fat, 20g carbohydrates, 11g protein, 4g fiber, 6g sugar

MISO SPREAD

Active time: 10 minutes | **Cook time:** N/A | **Yield:** 4 servings

INGREDIENTS:

2 tsps extra-virgin olive oil

1 tbsp lemon juice

1 tsp chili oil

½ cup cucumber, peeled, seeded, and diced

½ cup water

1 cup white, yellow, or red miso

½ cup plain Greek yogurt

Miso is a Japanese thick paste made of fermented soybeans. It's high in protein and vitamins, and makes a great snack spread.

QUICK TIP: You might find red or white. While the taste is slightly different, you can use them interchangeably.

PREPARATION:

1. In a food processor, process all ingredients and pulse until well blended and smooth.
2. Serve immediately, or refrigerate for up to 4 days.

SERVING INFO: 110 calories, 6g fat, 7g carbohydrate, 7g protein, 3g fiber, 85mg sodium

EDAMAME DIP

Active time: 10 minutes | **Cook time:** 5 minutes | **Yield:** 4 servings

INGREDIENTS:

2 garlic cloves

1 cup water

2 cups frozen shelled edamame, thawed

½ tsp ground cumin

½ tsp salt

1 tbsp extra-virgin olive oil

2 tbsps lemon juice

¼ cup plain Greek yogurt

2 tbsps water

1 tbsp chopped fresh cilantro

Strange name, but a wonderful, healthy, nutritious dip made from edamame soybeans, which are picked when they are young and green, soft and edible. This bean is touted as a superfood. It will punch up fiber, protein, vitamin, and mineral content in your diet.

QUICK TIP: Make this flavorful dip a day or two in advance, and store it covered tightly in the fridge.

PREPARATION:
1. Bring 2 cups water to a boil; add edamame, and boil 5 minutes. Drain.
2. Combine edamame, garlic, cumin, salt, olive oil, lemon juice in a food processor, and pulse until smooth. Add 2 tbsps of water if necessary. Garnish mixture with the chopped cilantro and serve.

CAULIFLOWER WHITE BEAN DIP

Active time: 5 minutes | **Cook time:** N/A | **Yield:** 4 servings

INGREDIENTS:

1 small head cauliflower, trimmed and cut into bite-sized florets

5 garlic cloves, peeled and minced

1 small can cannellini beans, rinsed and drained

½ cup Italian parsley, minced

1 tsp lemon zest

1 tbsp extra-virgin olive oil

1 tbsp lemon juice

salt and pepper to taste

Hummus, the garbanzo bean dip (see page 219), is widely enjoyed in all the countries bordering the Mediterranean Sea. While hummus is the star, its white bean cousin, is also popular in those parts of the world, and for good reason. It's delicious! So enjoy this tasty treat as the base of this recipe for cauliflower dip.

QUICK TIP: Cannellini beans are the basic ingredients. But you can experiment with other beans, too, such as garbanzo, pinto, navy, and so on.

PREPARATION:

1. Preheat oven to 400° (200°c).
2. On a baking sheet, toss cauliflower and garlic with oil; season with salt and pepper. Roast until cauliflower is tender and browned, about 25 minutes.
3. In a food processor, combine cauliflower, garlic, beans, parsley, lemon zest and juice. Process until smooth. Add a bit of cold water if necessary. Salt and pepper to taste. Serve.

INDEX

-A-

Alinat, Gui, 11–12
Almond butter
Easy Granola Bar, 217
Almond flour
Chicken Pot Pie, 99
Skinny Pigs in a Blanket, 85
Almonds
Banana-Quinoa Porridge, 43
Easy Granola Bar, 217
Roquefort, Peach, and Almond Salad, 67
Steel-Cut Oatmeal and Fruits, 37
Anchovies
Healthy Caesar Salad, 63
Traditional Pasta Putanesca, 167
Appetizers, 49–89
Basic Vinaigrette, 87
Broccoli Cheese Soup, 57
Caprese Salad with Burrata, 65
Carrot-Ginger Soup, 55
Cauliflower Tabouleh, 74–75
Chicken Noodle Soup, 61
Fat-Burning Salad Dressing, 89
French Onion Soup, 58–59
Grilled Corn & Summer Vegetable Salad, 73
Healthy Caesar Salad, 63
Healthy Chicken Wings, 83
Mexican Three Bean Salad, 71
Overnight Savory Oatmeal, 79
Roquefort, Peach, and Almond Salad, 67
Skinny Pigs in a Blanket, 85
Southwestern Egg Rolls, 81

Spinach, Roasted Fennel and Grapefruit Salad, 69
Supercharged Guacamole, 51
Tuscan Minestrone, 53
Waldorf Salad, 77
Apples
Pork Tenderloin Roast with Caramelized Apples, 133
Waldorf Salad, 77
Apricots
Marinated Fruit Salad, 45
Asparagus
Fresh and Bright Pasta Primavera, 164–165
Avocados
Cottage Cheese-Stuffed Avocado, 223
Huevos Rancheros, 30–31
Supercharged Guacamole, 51

-B-

Baked Eggs with Salsa Verde, 35
Bananas
Banana-Quinoa Porridge, 43
Belgian Waffles, 19
Easy Banana Bread, 23
Old-Fashioned Pancakes, 21
Basic Vinaigrette, 87
Basil
Caprese Salad with Burrata, 65
Chicken Noodle Soup, 61
Classic Pasta a la Norma, 161
Fresh and Bright Pasta Primavera, 164–165
The New Alfredo Sauce, 163
Roasted Butternut Squash and Hazelnut, 189

Tuscan Minestrone, 53
Beans. *See* Black beans; Cannellini beans; Garbanzo beans; Green beans; Kidney beans; Refried beans
Beat the Beetroot, 195
Beef. *See also* Ground beef
Beef and Broccoli Stir-Fry, 117
Best. Steak. Ever., 119–120
Make-Your-Own Jerky, 221
Beefsteak tomatoes
Caprese Salad with Burrata, 65
Salmon Baked in Foil, 150
Supercharged Guacamole, 51
Beets
Beat the Beetroot, 195
Rainbow Root Vegetable Roast, 191
Belgian Waffles, 19
Bison
Supermeatballs, 126–127
Black beans
Mexican Chile Rellenos, 157
Mexican Three Bean Salad, 71
Southwestern Egg Rolls, 81
Blueberries
Blueberry Muffins, 25
Steel-Cut Oatmeal and Fruits, 37
Blue cheese
Healthy Chicken Wings, 83
Brazil nuts
Toasted Brazil Nuts, 213
Breads
Blueberry Muffins, 25
Easy Banana Bread, 23
Breakfast, 17–47

Baked Eggs with Salsa Verde, 35
Banana-Quinoa Porridge, 43
Belgian Waffles, 19
Blueberry Muffins, 25
Easy Banana Bread, 23
French Toast, 29
The Good Wrap, 41
Huevos Rancheros, 30–31
Marinated Fruit Salad, 45
My Eggs Florentine, 38–39
Old-Fashioned Pancakes, 21
The Real Scramble, 47
Spanish Tortilla, 33
Spinach and Tomato Frittata, 27
Steel-Cut Oatmeal and Fruits, 37
Broccoli
Beef and Broccoli Stir-Fry, 117
Broccoli and Spinach Casserole, 207
Broccoli Cheese Soup, 57
No-Bread Cheese Sandwich, 175
Ultra-Fast Tilapia Bake, 153
Brussels sprouts, Caramelized, 201
Buckwheat flour
Belgian Waffles, 19
Blueberry Muffins, 25
Green Bean Casserole, 199
Old-Fashioned Pancakes, 21
Burrata, 65
Buttermilk
Healthy Southern Fried Chicken, 112

Cabbage
Leafy Greens Enchilada, 173
Tuscan Minestrone, 53
Calories, empty, 14
Cannellini beans
Cauliflower White Bean Dip, 229
Tuscan Minestrone, 53
Capers
Chicken Piccata, 103
Traditional Pasta Putanesca, 167
Caprese Salad with Burrata, 65
Caramelized Brussels Sprouts, 201
Carrots
Braised Pork with White Wine and Carrots, 135
Carrot-Ginger Soup, 55
Carrots and Homemade Hummus, 219
Chicken Noodle Soup, 61
Chicken Pot Pie, 99
Rainbow Root Vegetable Roast, 191
Sweet and Spicy Roast Pork, 137
Tuscan Minestrone, 53
Cauliflower
Cauliflower Tabouleh, 74–75
Cauliflower White Bean Dip, 229
Shrimp and Grits, 148
Ultra-Fast Tilapia Bake, 153
Celery
Chicken Noodle Soup, 61
Chicken Pot Pie, 99
Healthy Chicken Wings, 83
Tuscan Minestrone, 53
Waldorf Salad, 77
Chard
Leafy Greens Enchilada, 173
Lean and Green Baked Ziti, 169
Cheddar cheese
No-Bread Cheese Sandwich, 175
Cheese. See Blue cheese; Cheddar cheese; Cottage cheese; Feta cheese; Goat cheese; Gouda cheese; Monterey Jack cheese; Mozzarella cheese; Neufchâtel cheese; Parmesan cheese; Parmigiano-Reggiano cheese; Queso fresco; Ricotta cheese; Swiss cheese
Cherry tomatoes
Caprese Salad with Burrata, 65
Chicken
Bourbon Chicken, 93
Chicken Cordon Bleu, 101
Chicken Marsala, 109
Chicken Noodle Soup, 61
Chicken Piccata, 103
Chicken Pot Pie, 99
Chicken Teriyaki, 107
Chicken Tikka Marsala, 104–105
Family Chicken Nuggets, 94–95
Healthy Chicken Wings, 83
Healthy Southern Fried Chicken, 112–113
Homemade Rotisserie Chicken, 97
Orange Chicken, 111
Southwestern Egg Rolls, 81
Chicken broth
Braised Pork with White Wine and Carrots, 135
Broccoli Cheese Soup, 57
Carrot-Ginger Soup, 55
Chicken Cordon Bleu, 101
Chicken Noodle Soup, 61
Chicken Pot Pie, 99
Fresh and Bright Pasta Primavera, 164–165
Pork Thai Curry, 139
Tuscan Minestrone, 53
Chiles
Leafy Greens Enchilada, 173
Chili, Black Kale, 123
Chives
Caprese Salad with Burrata, 65

Chocolate
Strawberries and
Chocolate, 215
Cilantro
Mexican Three Bean
Salad, 71
Coconut
Coconut Shrimp, 145
Wilted Black Kale with
Coconut, 205
Coconut flour
Belgian Waffles, 19
Blueberry Muffins, 25
Braised Pork with White
Wine and Carrots, 135
British Fish and Chips, 155
Broccoli Cheese Soup, 57
Chicken Cordon Bleu, 101
Chicken Marsala, 109
Chicken Piccata, 103
Chicken Pot Pie, 99
Coconut Shrimp, 145
Easy Banana Bread, 23
Family Chicken Nuggets,
94–95
Fat-Burning Pizza, 177
French Onion Soup, 58–59
Healthy Southern Fried
Chicken, 112
Mac and Cheese and Kale,
194–195
My Eggs Florentine, 38–39
The New Alfredo Sauce,
163
Old-Fashioned Pancakes,
21
Orange Chicken, 111
Skinny Pigs in a Blanket,
85
Zucchini au Gratin, 186–
187
Coconut milk
Chicken Tikka Marsala,
104–105
Corn
Grilled Corn & Summer
Vegetable Salad, 73
Leafy Greens Enchilada,
173
Southwestern Egg Rolls,
81

Cottage Cheese-Stuffed
Avocado, 223
Couscous
Cauliflower Tabouleh,
74–75
Cranberries
Cauliflower Tabouleh,
74–75
Easy Granola Bar, 217
Overnight Savory
Oatmeal, 79
Crispy Sweet Potato Fries,
181
Cucumbers
Miso Spread, 225

- D -

Dates
Easy Granola Bar, 217
Deep-frying, 15
Desserts
Easy Granola Bar, 217
Strawberries and
Chocolate, 215

- E -

Easy Banana Bread, 23
Easy Granola Bar, 217
Edamame
Edamame Dip, 227
Fresh and Bright Pasta
Primavera, 164–165
Mexican Three Bean
Salad, 71
Eggplant
Classic Pasta a la Norma,
161
Eggs/egg whites
Baked Eggs with Salsa
Verde, 35
British Fish and Chips, 155
Broccoli and Spinach
Casserole, 207
Coconut Shrimp, 145
Family Chicken Nuggets,
94–95
Fat-Burning Pizza, 177
French Toast, 29
The Good Wrap, 41
Hard-Boiled Eggs, 211

Healthy Southern Fried
Chicken, 112
Hearty Yellow Squash
Casserole, 183
Huevos Rancheros, 30–31
My Eggs Florentine, 38–39
No-Bread Cheese
Sandwich, 175
The Real Scramble, 47
Spanish Tortilla, 33
Spinach and Tomato
Frittata, 27
Empty calories, 14
**Enchilada, Leafy Greens,
173**
Equipment, 16

- F -

Fat-Burning Salad Dressing,
89
Fennel, Spinach, Roasted,
and Grapefruit Salad,
69
Feta cheese
Beat the Beetroot, 195
Grilled Corn & Summer
Vegetable Salad, 73
Fiber, 14
Fish and seafood
British Fish and Chips, 155
Coconut Shrimp, 145
Grilled Marinated Shrimp,
143
Grilled Salmon and
Mango Salsa, 147
Salmon Baked in Foil,
150–151
Shrimp and Grits, 148–149
Simple Mahi with Sesame
Soy Sauce, 141
Ultra-Fast Tilapia Bake,
153
Flaxseed
Belgian Waffles, 19
Flour. *See also* Almond
flour; Buckwheat flour;
Coconut flour; Whole-
grain flour
replacing refined, 15
French Onion Soup, 58–59
Salisbury Steak, 115

French Toast, 29

Frittata, Spinach and Tomato, 27

 -G-

Garam masala
Chicken Tikka Masala, 104–105

Garbanzo beans
Carrots and Homemade Hummus, 219

Ginger
Carrot-Ginger Soup, 55

Goat cheese
The Good Wrap, 41
The Good Wrap, 41

Gouda cheese
Mac and Cheese and Kale, 194–195

Grapefruit
Spinach, Roasted Fennel and Grapefruit Salad, 69

Greek yogurt
Broccoli and Spinach Casserole, 207
Chicken Pot Pie, 99
Chicken Tikka Masala, 104–105
Edamame Dip, 227
Green Bean Casserole, 199
Healthy Caesar Salad, 63
Healthy Chicken Wings, 83
Lean and Green Baked Ziti, 169
Miso Spread, 225
Overnight Savory Oatmeal, 79
Skinny Pigs in a Blanket, 85
Steel-Cut Oatmeal and Fruits, 37
Waldorf Salad, 77
Green Bean Casserole, 199
Grilled Corn & Summer Vegetable Salad, 73
Grits, Shrimp and, 148

Ground beef
Black Kale Chili, 123
Cuban Picadillo, 129
Lean and Green Baked

Ziti, 169
Mexican Chile Rellenos, 157
Old-Fashioned Meatloaf, 125
Salisbury Steak, 115
Supermeatballs, 126–127

Guacamole, Supercharged, 51

 -H-

Ham
Chicken Cordon Bleu, 101
Spanish Tortilla, 33
Spinach and Tomato Frittata, 27
Hard-Boiled Eggs, 211

Hazelnuts
Roasted Butternut Squash and Hazelnut, 189
Healthy Caesar Salad, 63
Healthy Chicken Wings, 83
Hearty Yellow Squash Casserole, 183

Hot dogs
Skinny Pigs in a Blanket, 85
Huevos Rancheros, 30–31

Hummus
T he Good Wrap, 41

 -I-

Ingredients
organic, 14
shocking, 15

Italian sausage
Cuban Picadillo, 129

-J-

Jalapeno peppers
Huevos Rancheros, 30–31
Mexican Chile Rellenos, 157
Southwestern Egg Rolls, 81
Wilted Black Kale with Coconut, 205

 -K-

Kale
Black Kale Chili, 123
Kids' Fav Kale Chips, 203
Leafy Greens Enchilada, 173
Mac and Cheese and Kale, 194–195
Shrimp and Grits, 148
Supercharged Guacamole, 51
Wilted Black Kale with Coconut, 205

Kidney beans
Black Kale Chili, 123
Mexican Three Bean Salad, 71
Kids' Fav Kale Chips, 203

Kiwi
Marinated Fruit Salad, 45

-L-

Lemons
Cauliflower Tabouleh, 74–75
Cauliflower White Bean Dip, 229
Grilled Corn & Summer Vegetable Salad, 73
Grilled Marinated Shrimp, 143
Sweet and Spicy Roast Pork, 137

Lettuce
Healthy Caesar Salad, 63
Roquefort, Peach, and Almond Salad, 67

Limes
Supercharged Guacamole, 51

 -M-

Mac and Cheese and Kale, 194–195
Mahi-Mahi, Simple, with Sesame Soy Sauce, 141

Main courses, 91–177
Beef and Broccoli Stir-Fry, 117

Best. Steak. Ever, 119–120

Black Kale Chili, 123

Bourbon Chicken, 93

Braised Pork with White Wine and Carrots, 135

British Fish and Chips, 155

Chicken Cordon Bleu, 101

Chicken Marsala, 109

Chicken Piccata, 103

Chicken Pot Pie, 99

Chicken Teriyaki, 107

Chicken Tikka Masala, 104–105

Chile Bolognese, 159

Classic Pasta a la Norma, 161

Coconut Shrimp, 145

Country-Style BBQ Ribs, 131

Cuban Picadillo, 129

Family Chicken Nuggets, 94–95

Fat-Burning Pizza, 177

Fresh and Bright Pasta Primavera, 164–165

Grilled Marinated Shrimp, 143

Grilled Salmon and Mango Salsa, 147

Healthy Southern Fried Chicken, 112–113

Homemade Rotisserie Chicken, 97

Leafy Greens Enchilada, 173

Lean and Green Baked Ziti, 169

Mexican Chile Rellenos, 157

The New Alfredo Sauce, 163

No-Bread Grilled Cheese Sandwich, 175

Old-Fashioned Meatloaf, 125

Orange Chicken, 111

Pork Tenderloin Roast with Caramelized Apples, 133

Pork Thai Curry, 139

Salisbury Steak, 115

Salmon Baked in Foil, 150

Shrimp and Grits, 148–149

Simple Mahi with Sesame Soy Sauce, 141

Spinach and Ricotta Lasagna, 171

Supermeatballs, 126–127

Sweet and Spicy Roast Pork, 137

Traditional Pasta Puttanesca, 167

Ultra-Fast Tilapia Bake, 153

Make-Your-Own Jerky, 221

Mangoes

Grilled Salmon and Mango Salsa, 147

Marinated Fruit Salad, 45

Marion, Joel, 11

Mediterranean Diet, 12

Mexican Chile Rellenos Chile Bolognese, 159

Mexican Three Bean Salad, 71

Miso Spread, 225

Monterey Jack cheese

Southwestern Egg Rolls, 81

Mozzarella cheese

Broccoli and Spinach Casserole, 207

French Onion Soup, 58–59

Green Bean Casserole, 199

Hearty Yellow Squash Casserole, 183

Leafy Greens Enchilada, 173

Lean and Green Baked Ziti, 169

No-Bread Cheese Sandwich, 175

Spinach and Ricotta Lasagna, 171

Supermeatballs, 126–127

Zucchini au Gratin, 186–187

Muffins, Blueberry, 25

My Eggs Florentine, 38–39

Neufchâtel cheese

My Eggs Florentine, 38–39

Not-so French Fries, 193

Nuts. *See* Almonds; Brazil nuts; Peanuts; Pistachios; Walnuts

Oats

Easy Granola Bar, 217

Overnight Savory Oatmeal, 79

Steel-Cut Oatmeal and Fruits, 37

Old-Fashioned Pancakes, 21

Olive oil, 15

Olives

Braised Pork with White Wine and Carrots, 135

Spinach, Roasted Fennel and Grapefruit Salad, 69

Traditional Pasta Putanesca, 167

Onions. *See also* Red onions

Beef and Broccoli Stir-Fry, 117

Black Kale Chili, 123

Broccoli and Spinach Casserole, 207

Broccoli Cheese Soup, 57

Caramelized Brussels Sprouts, 201

Carrot-Ginger Soup, 55

Cuban Picadillo, 129

French Onion Soup, 58–59

Fresh and Bright Pasta Primavera, 164–165

Green Bean Casserole, 199

Lean and Green Baked Ziti, 169

Mexican Chile Rellenos, 157

Old-Fashioned Meatloaf, 125

Pork Thai Curry, 139

Salmon Baked in Foil, 150

Spanish Tortilla, 33

Spinach and Ricotta Lasagna, 171

Supermeatballs, 126–127

Sweet and Spicy Roast Pork, 137

Tuscan Minestrone, 53
Zucchini au Gratin, 186–187
Organic ingredients, 14
Overnight Savory Oatmeal, 79

Pacific cod
British Fish and Chips, 155
Pancetta
Supermeatballs, 126–127
Parmesan cheese
British Fish and Chips, 155
Mac and Cheese and Kale, 194–195
The New Alfredo Sauce, 163
Spinach and Ricotta Lasagna, 171
Parmigiano-Reggiano cheese
Broccoli Cheese Soup, 57
Chile Bolognese, 159
Classic Pasta a la Norma, 161
Fresh and Bright Pasta Primavera, 164–165
Healthy Caesar Salad, 63
Lean and Green Baked Ziti, 169
No-Bread Cheese Sandwich, 175
Shrimp and Grits, 148
Supermeatballs, 126–127
Tuscan Minestrone, 53
Parsnips
Not-so-French Fries, 193
Rainbow Root Vegetable Roast, 191
Pasta. *See* Whole-grain pasta
Pasta al dente, 14
Peaches
Marinated Fruit Salad, 45
Roquefort, Peach, and Almond Salad, 67
Peanuts
Pork Thai Curry, 139
Peas. *See also* Sugar-snap peas
Chicken Pot Pie, 99

Fresh and Bright Pasta Primavera, 164–165
Peppers. *See* Jalapeno peppers; Poblano peppers; Red bell peppers
Pineapple
Marinated Fruit Salad, 45
Pistachios
Beat the Beetroot, 195
Cauliflower Tabouleh, 74–75
Overnight Savory Oatmeal, 79
Poblano peppers
Grilled Corn & Summer Vegetable Salad, 73
Mexican Chile Rellenos, 157
Pork. *See also* Ham; Pancetta
Braised Pork with White Wine and Carrots, 135
Country-Style BBQ Ribs, 131
Pork Tenderloin Roast with Caramelized Apples, 133
Pork Thai Curry, 139
Supermeatballs, 126–127
Sweet and Spicy Roast Pork, 137

Queso fresco
Baked Eggs with Salsa Verde, 35
Huevos Rancheros, 30–31
Mexican Chile Rellenos, 157
Quinoa, Banana-, Porridge, 43

Rainbow Root Vegetable Roast, 191
The Real Scramble, 47
Red bell peppers
Mexican Three Bean Salad, 71
Southwestern Egg Rolls, 81

Ultra-Fast Tilapia Bake, 153
Red onions
The Good Wrap, 41
Grilled Salmon and Mango Salsa, 147
Mexican Three Bean Salad, 71
Supercharged Guacamole, 51
Refried beans
Huevos Rancheros, 30–31
Ricotta cheese
Spinach and Ricotta Lasagna, 171
Supermeatballs, 126–127
Roasted Butternut Squash and Hazelnut, 189
Roasted Faux Fries, 185
Roquefort, Peach, and Almond Salad, 67
Rutabaga
Pork Thai Curry, 139
Rainbow Root Vegetable Roast, 191
Roasted Faux Fries, 185
Spanish Tortilla, 33

Salad dressings
Basic Vinaigrette, 87
Fat-Burning Salad Dressing, 89
Salads
Caprese Salad with Burrata, 65
Cauliflower Tabouleh, 74–75
Grilled Corn & Summer Vegetable Salad, 73
Healthy Caesar Salad, 63
Marinated Fruit Salad, 45
Mexican Three Bean Salad, 71
Roquefort, Peach, and Almond Salad, 67
Spinach, Roasted Fennel and Grapefruit Salad, 69
Waldorf Salad, 77

Salmon
Grilled Salmon and
Mango Salsa, 147
Salmon Baked in Foil, 150
Salsa Verde, Baked Eggs
with, 35
San Marzano Tomatoes
Classic Pasta a la Norma,
161
Lean and Green Baked
Ziti, 169
Spinach and Ricotta
Lasagna, 171
Supermeatballs, 126–127
Traditional Pasta
Putanesca, 167
Seafood. *See* Fish and
seafood
Shrimp
Coconut Shrimp, 145
Grilled Marinated Shrimp,
143
Shrimp and Grits, 148
Sides, 179–207
Beat the Beetroot, 195
Broccoli and Spinach
Casserole, 207
Caramelized Brussels
Sprouts, 201
Crispy Sweet Potato Fries,
181
Green Bean Casserole, 199
Hearty Yellow Squash
Casserole, 183
Kids' Fav Kale Chips, 203
Mac and Cheese and Kale,
194–195
Not-so French Fries, 193
Rainbow Root Vegetable
Roast, 191
Roasted Butternut Squash
and Hazelnut, 189
Roasted Faux Fries, 185
Wilted Black Kale with
Coconut, 205
Zucchini au Gratin, 186–
187
Skinny Pigs in a Blanket, 85
Snacks, 209–229
Carrots and Homemade
Hummus, 219
Cauliflower White Bean

Dip, 229
Cottage Cheese-Stuffed
Avocado, 223
Easy Granola Bar, 217
Edamame Dip, 229
Hard-Boiled Eggs, 211
Make-Your-Own Jerky, 221
Miso Spread, 225
Strawberry and Chocolate,
215
Toasted Brazil Nuts, 213
Soups
Broccoli Cheese Soup, 57
Carrot-Ginger Soup, 55
Chicken Noodle Soup, 61
French Onion Soup, 58–59
Tuscan Minestrone, 53
Southwestern Egg Rolls,
81
Spanish Tortilla, 33
Spinach
Broccoli and Spinach
Casserole, 207
The Good Wrap, 41
Lean and Green Baked
Ziti, 169
My Eggs Florentine, 38–39
The Real Scramble, 47
Southwestern Egg Rolls,
81
Spinach, Roasted Fennel
and Grapefruit Salad,
69
Spinach and Ricotta
Lasagna, 171
Spinach and Tomato
Frittata, 27
Squash
Hearty Yellow Squash
Casserole, 183
Roasted Butternut Squash
and Hazelnut, 189
Sriracha sauce
Healthy Chicken Wings,
83
Steel-Cut Oatmeal and
Fruits, 37
Stir-Fry, Beef and Broccoli,
117
Strawberries
Marinated Fruit Salad, 45
Strawberries and

Chocolate, 215
Sugars, replacing, 15
Sugar snap peas
Fresh and Bright Pasta
Primavera, 164–165
Sundried tomatoes
The Good Wrap, 41
Sundried tomatoes
The Real Scramble, 47
Supercharged Guacamole,
51
Sweet potatoes
Crispy Sweet Potato Fries,
181
Swiss cheese
Chicken Cordon Bleu, 101

-T-

Tahini
Carrots and Homemade
Hummus, 219
Tilapia, Ultra-Fast, Bake,
153
Toasted Brazil Nuts, 213
Tomatoes. *See also*
Beefsteak
tomatoes;
Cherry
tomatoes;
San Marzano
Tomatoes;
Sundried
tomatoes
Black Kale Chili, 123
Cauliflower Tabouleh,
74–75
Chicken Tikka Masala,
104–105
Chile Bolognese, 159
Cuban Picadillo, 129
Huevos Rancheros, 30–31
Leafy Greens Enchilada,
173
Mexican Chile Rellenos,
157
Spinach and Tomato
Frittata, 27
Tuscan Minestrone, 53
Tortillas
Baked Eggs with Salsa
Verde, 35

The Good Wrap, 41
Huevos Rancheros, 30–31
Leafy Greens Enchilada, 173
Southwestern Egg Rolls, 81

Turkey
Spinach and Ricotta Lasagna, 171

Turnips
Rainbow Root Vegetable Roast, 191
Tuscan Minestrone, 53

Veal
Supermeatballs, 126–127

Waldorf Salad, 77

Walnuts
Grilled Corn & Summer Vegetable Salad, 73
Waldorf Salad, 77

Whole-grain bread
French Onion Soup, 58–59
French Toast, 29

Whole-grain cereal
British Fish and Chips, 155
Broccoli and Spinach

Casserole, 207
Family Chicken Nuggets, 94–95
Green Bean Casserole, 199
Healthy Caesar Salad, 63
Healthy Southern Fried Chicken, 112
Hearty Yellow Squash Casserole, 183
Mac and Cheese and Kale, 194–195
Old-Fashioned Meatloaf, 125
Supermeatballs, 126–127
Zucchini au Gratin, 186–187

Whole-grain flour
Belgian Waffles, 19
Chicken Pot Pie, 99
Skinny Pigs in a Blanket, 85

Whole-grain pasta
Chicken Noodle Soup, 61
Chile Bolognese, 159
Classic Pasta a la Norma, 161
Fresh and Bright Pasta Primavera, 164–165
Lean and Green Baked Ziti, 169
Mac and Cheese and Kale, 194–195

The New Alfredo Sauce, 163
Spinach and Ricotta Lasagna, 171
Traditional Pasta Puttanesca, 167
Tuscan Minestrone, 53
Wilted Black Kale with Coconut, 205

Wine
Braised Pork with White Wine and Carrots, 135
Chicken Marsala, 109
French Onion Soup, 58–59
Mexican Chile Rellenos, 157

Wraps
The Good Wrap, 41

Yogurt. *See* Greek yogurt

-Z-

Zucchini
Fresh and Bright Pasta Primavera, 164–165
Grilled Corn & Summer Vegetable Salad, 73
Zucchini au Gratin, 186–187

BIOGRAPHY

GUI ALINAT is a Tampa-based American Culinary Federation Certified Executive Chef, published food writer and the owner of Artisan Boutique Catering.

Born, raised and classically trained as a chef on the Mediterranean coast of France, he traveled extensively, working in restaurants around the world. Settling in Florida in 1999, he has been catering high-end private events with his own company for the last 15 years. With an exclusive client base and media recognition, his team became a recognized landmark in the Tampa Bay culinary scene. Chef Gui promotes an active lifestyle and focuses on sound nutrition. He believes that fresh and tasty food is resolutely compatible with fat loss and bodybuilding alike. His culinary style can be best described as nutritious and healthy, with strong influences from the lifestyle of the Mediterranean region, where he grew up.

He lives in Florida with his wife Carissa and their five children.

To connect with Chef Gui:
Web: www.earlytorise.com/chef
Instagram: chefgui
LinkedIn: Gui Alinat, CEC
Pinterest: Chef Gui Alinat

ALSO BY CHEF GUI ALINAT:
The Chef's Repertoire, an award-winning reference culinary book available on Amazon.